Power, Providen
and Personality

Also by Walter Brueggemann

Hope Within History
In Man We Trust:
    The Neglected Side of Biblical Faith
The Bible Makes Sense

Tradition for Crisis: Hosea
Genesis (Interpretation)
First and Second Samuel (Interpretation)
I Kings (Knox Preaching Guides)
II Kings (Knox Preaching Guides)

Edited by Walter Brueggemann

I Am Yahweh, by Walther Zimmerli

Power, Providence, and Personality

Biblical Insight Into Life and Ministry

Walter Brueggemann

Westminster/John Knox Press
Louisville, Kentucky

Scripture quotations from the Revised Standard Version of the Bible are copyrighted 1946, 1952, ©1971, 1973 by the Division of Christian Education of the National Council of the Churches of Christ in the U.S.A. and are used by permission.

Book design by Gene Harris

First edition

Published by Westminster/John Knox Press
Louisville, Kentucky

PRINTED IN THE UNITED STATES OF AMERICA

9 8 7 6 5 4 3 2 1

Library of Congress Cataloging-in-Publication Data

Brueggemann, Walter.
    Power, providence, and personality : biblical insight into life
and ministry / Walter Brueggemann. — 1st ed.
        p.   cm.
    Includes bibliographical references.
    ISBN 0-664-25138-2

    1. Bible. O.T. Samuel—Criticism, interpretation, etc.
2. Narration in the Bible. 3. Pastoral theology. I. Title.
BS1325.2.B79 1990
222'.406—dc20   90-32247
                                                         CIP

With thanks to the
faculty of
Episcopal Seminary of Alexandria

Contents

Preface

This series of studies is a spin-off of my work on *First and Second Samuel* to be published this year in the Interpretation series under the imprint of John Knox Press. I have sought to elaborate and extrapolate from my exegesis there to make the text more accessible for the practice of the church. Two of these studies have received more detailed and technical discussion in my work. On chapter 3, see "Narrative Intentionality in I Samuel 29," *Journal for the Study of the Old Testament* 43 (1989): 21–35, and on chapter 4, see "2 Samuel 21–24: An Appendix of Deconstruction?" *Catholic Biblical Quarterly* 50 (1988): 383–397.

Two concerns have been uppermost in my mind in preparing these studies. First, I have tried to pay attention to newer methods of interpretation that go under the general rubric of "literary criticism." I have no doubt that in such methods, still largely unrecognized in the church and among ministers, there are enormous gains both concerning how texts may be understood (literary criticism) and concerning what happens in the act of interpretation (literary theory). In the books of Samuel these methods focus on "narrative strategy," which attends to what the narrator is trying to *do* in the text. I have tried to show how "narrative strategy" in the text is worth notice, because it may converge with or critique the narrative strategy through which we try to *do* something with our lives.

Second, I am aware that the "consumers" of the text in the church do not just sit around and read texts (which would not be a bad thing), but have tasks that must be performed on a daily basis. It is the case, however, that the ministerial tasks in the church have been largely cut off from the authorization and scrutiny of scripture. On the whole, scripture is thought to be directly relevant only to preaching, but not to such other matters as counseling, liturgy, education, and management. In response to that breach between text and practice, I have sought to carry my exposition toward specific tasks of ministry, suggesting that much of our uncertainty or excessive certainty or ineffectiveness or fraudulence in ministry is because we have not understood how scripture provides a context and critical principle for all our ministerial work.

These studies have been offered as lectures in a number of places in various recensions and stages of development. These include the Schmeichen Lectures at Eden Theological Seminary (my home base where I first offered them), the Sprinkle Lectures at Atlantic Christian College, the Zabriskie Lectures at Episcopal Seminary in Alexandria, Virginia, Pastoral Lectures at Luther Northwestern Theological Seminary (St. Paul), the Earl Lectures at Pacific School of Religion, the Walter Binns Lectures at William Jewell College, and the Virgil H. and Irene R. Todd Lectures at Memphis Theological Seminary. In all these places I have been graciously received and wondrously hosted, and I thank my several hosts for their thoughtfulness, generosity, and good food and drink. I am glad to dedicate this little book to my colleagues at Episcopal Seminary (and especially to my friend Murray Newman), who graced me with an honorary degree.

This manuscript has been a long time developing with many layers of work. Its completion has been possible because of the typing in turn of Richard Deibert, Bud Brainerd, and finally Donna LaGrasso. Ms. LaGrasso is endlessly steadfast and persistent in bringing my random thoughts and sentences to presentable form, and I am grateful. Finally I am grateful to Davis Perkins in his new work at Westminster/John Knox Press for his willingness to take on this manuscript and for his care and attentiveness in bringing it to fruition. I will be pleased if these studies contribute to the new engagement of "mainline" U.S. churches with scripture. There are indeed ways of nurture and discipline from scripture to which we have paid little attention, and that to our impoverishment. Our reengagement is a verse and a sentence at a time, and I am glad to take up these verses and contribute my sentences.

Columbia Theological Seminary   Walter Brueggemann

1

An Artistic Disclosure
in Three Dimensions

The task of theological interpretation of scripture is profoundly complex. The subject matter, focus, and perspective of biblical texts are difficult to discern and articulate because our conventional categories of theology do not work very well with the texts. Moreover, the reason the text is so complex is that the experience of life and faith mediated in the text is itself incredibly complicated. The Bible does not want to slot life-experiences easily into any of our logical, conventional categories but wants to exhibit the strange and crucial convergences and interfaces that matter most for our life and for our faith.

My work in 1 and 2 Samuel has led me to articulate this nonnegotiable complexity under the three themes of power, providence, and personality. I have settled on these themes because together they express the attractive reality of David, the hidden but forceful presence of Yahweh, and the revolutionary cultural situation in which both David and Yahweh are presented. I pursue this complexity here because I judge this same complexity to be present in and important for our life and faith. Let me explain what I mean by the three themes of power, providence, and personality.

Power. I use the word "power" to speak about the flow of social forces that include the raw power of technology and the relentless, shameless pressure of ideology. There can be no doubt that such ideological and technological forces are at work in and around the text of Samuel. The most obvious appearance of such social forces is in the dispute about kingship between the "pro-monarchial" and "anti-monarchial" forces. These powerful opinions are not simply voices of personal preference but express powerful vested interests.

As the story of the monarchy develops, the various challenges to David, the continuing power of the Saulide party, (those who continued to be loyal to Saul), and the enduring dispute of north and south all reflect partisan social interests. Moreover, these interests are not simply geographical and political; no doubt they express economic conflict and a dispute over social, religious power and influence. The hidden purposes of God are no doubt powerful, but their work must be done in the presence of and through these interests which are determined and stubborn and not at all deferential. Those factors tend not to be explicit in the text itself; their hiddenness in the text is part of their power.

On the whole, scripture study has been innocent of such matters. Only recently, especially in the work of Norman Gottwald,[1] have we arrived at the methodological self-awareness about scripture necessary to see that the texts operate in relation to powerful social systems that may use individual agents but are larger and more powerful than those individuals. In the books of Samuel, what I call "power" of course refers to pro- and anti-monarchial political opinion, but it refers as well to ideological groups who owned land or wanted land reform, to social organization committed to the centralization of power, to the management of an accumulated surplus of value and the emergence of a bureaucracy, and to a monopolistic priesthood. Those strange new developments in Israel posed an enormous challenge to old, tough egalitarian social opinion.[2]

---

[1]Norman Gottwald, *The Tribes of Yahweh* (Maryknoll, N.Y.: Orbis Books, 1979).

[2]For one attractive analysis of this old egalitarian opinion, see Martin Cohen, "The Role of the Shilonite Priesthood in the United Monarchy of Ancient Israel," *Hebrew Union College Annual* 36 (1965): 59–98.

Providence. By "providence" I mean the hidden, patient, sovereign enactment of God's overriding purpose beyond the will and choice of human agents. There is no doubt that Yahweh's providential sovereignty is operative in the Samuel narrative and is a main concern of the narrator. That providential intention is focused on the person of David, on his emergence in the historical process, and on his slow, eventual, but certain ascent to the throne of Israel. The process whereby David becomes king is in part a matter of good fortune and shrewd human strategies. Clearly, however, around good fortune and shrewd strategy there hovers another purpose, the purpose of Yahweh. Already in the Song of Hannah (1 Sam. 2:10), the king is anticipated. Then the hidden anticipation of David is indicated in the theonomous statements of 1 Sam. 15:28 and 28:17. The narrative seems to be a working-out of this will of Yahweh, which is never flatly explicit but which surfaces at many places in the narrative. Karl Barth insightfully noted that the word providence is related to "provide," *pro-video*, to "see beforehand" what is needed.[3]

Scripture scholars have found that this hidden caring of God is more difficult to speak about than the obvious, direct intrusions of God we have come to call "God's mighty acts." On the one hand, it is difficult to know what one is looking for and spot it when it happens, because one does not want to credit everything to God or reduce God's providence to

[3]Karl Barth, *Church Dogmatics* III/3 (Edinburgh: T. & T. Clark, 1960), pp. 3, 35. In 1 Sam. 16:3, as the narrative prepares to identify David, Yahweh says to Samuel, "I will cause you to *see*." On providence in the David narrative, see the comment of David M. Gunn, *The Fate of King Saul, Journal for the Study of the Old Testament* Supp. 14 (Sheffield: JSOT Press, 1980), 115–116: "David is a *favourite* of Yahweh; Saul, on the other hand, appears as a victim. For David, Yahweh is 'Providence'; for Saul, Yahweh is 'Fate.'" It may be that Gunn has a more Enlightenment notion of providence than I would propose, but it is evident that Yahweh's hidden purpose is allied with David, as the narrative tells it. See the comment of Robert Polzin, *Samuel and the Deuteronomist: A Literary Study of the Deuteronomic History*, part 1: *1 Samuel* (San Francisco: Harper & Row, 1989), 269–270, n. 1.

luck or good fortune. On the other hand, even when we think we know what constitutes God's hidden care, it is difficult to find the right language, language that is not supernaturalist or direct or explanatory. We must find language that is as restrained and cunning as the discernment of the narrator. Whatever our problems may be in speaking of providence, however, it is clear that in the stories of Samuel there is another purpose at work beyond the pathology of Saul or the genius of David. We cannot speak about these narratives unless we dare to notice the hidden "purposiveness" that is relentless, yet beyond anyone's management or manipulation.

Personality. In the midst of providence, which is cunning but undeniable, and power, which is present but not always visible, we must in Samuel also speak of personality. Nowhere else in the Old Testament do we have personalities so nicely sketched as with Samuel, Saul, and David, and in lesser ways with Abner and Joab and Nathan. One can see their brilliance, courage, foolishness, shamelessness, and fidelity set down in the literature as models.

As one reads closely, however, amid the profound psychological sophistication of the narrative one also notices that there are varieties of David and Samuel and Saul, so that the personalities of these several characters are not so stable as they seemed, but are fluid literary sketches. Rather than explaining this fluidity by saying we have several sources, we are more likely now to conclude that we are dealing with literary constructs of personalities. (We extrapolate to conclude that if that is so in this text, perhaps everyone's personality is more nearly a literary construct or proposal than we had imagined.)[4]

The themes of power, providence, and personality correlate loosely with—and require us to ask questions concern-

---

[4]See my summary comments on the person as "world-maker" in *Israel's Praise: Doxology Against Idolatry and Ideology* (Philadelphia: Fortress Press, 1988), with attention to the work of Robert Kegan, Roy Schaffer, and D. W. Winnicott.

ing—sociology, theology, and literature. I am drawn by these three themes to ask about the convergence of *sociology* (power) that notices and attends to the conflict of interests; *theology* (providence) that is not too frontal; and *literature* (personality) that dares to utilize more than one strategy in its articulation. Thus a convergence of themes requires for our interpretation also a convergence of methods.[5]

The Disclosive Power of Narrative

It is demanding, and at times maddening, that one must speak about all three of these factors at the same time in a single convergence. We will of course never quite get the matters of power, providence, and personality all rightly balanced. We must consider, nonetheless, what perspective even stands a chance of speaking about all these factors in the text (and in our life) at the same time. If we wish to focus on power, we can do socioeconomic analysis, but most such social analysis finally explains (away) everything, and will never permit us to speak about providence. If we wish only to pursue the providential will of God, we may settle for theology, but theology has not done very well at taking into account the reality of power. In parallel fashion, much recent psychology is excessively analytical, so that everything except the crucial oddness of the person is discussed; or conversely, psychology is too much attracted to religious categories and is not open to the realities of social power.[6] When

[5]This convergence of themes in the David narrative has a striking parallel in the career of Ibn Saud, as it is portrayed by James W. Flanagan in *David's Social Drama: A Hologram of Israel's Early Iron Age,* Social World of Biblical Antiquity, 7 (Sheffield: Almond Press, 1988), 337–341. Flanagan organizes his summary statement around three times: (a) "Personal Metamorphoses," (b) "Systemic Change," and (c) "Religion and Change." These rubrics are closely parallel to my categories of personality, power, and providence. It is noteworthy that Flanagan's heading for this section of his analysis is "Similarities Between Ibn Saud and David."

[6]The phrases "excessively analytical" and "too much attracted to religious categories" refer respectively to the work and trajectories set in mo-

one chooses sociology that is too reductionist, theology that
is too frontal, or psychology that is analytical or religiously
romantic, one inevitably stacks the cards and misses too
much. In our usual interpretation of the text (and of our
life), our propensity has been to select one of these empha-
ses to the disregard of everything else.

I have been dazzled by the Samuel literature because in
that literature Israel practiced (I refrain from saying discov-
ered or invented) *an artistic rendering of social public reality*
that allows for convergences, tensions, and transitions without being excessively reductionist in any direction. Israel's
artistic rendering, which takes seriously power, providence,
and personality, is narrative that does not claim to be a descriptive report on social reality, that does not claim to be
eyewitness to personalities in dialogue, and that does not
claim to speak directly about God.

Israel's settlement on *narrative* as its preferred mode of
discourse is a remarkable decision about the nature of revelation and about the texture of social reality.[7] Israel's decision about narrative reflects the practical awareness that
what is said largely depends on *how* it is said.[8] This central
decision made in Israel poses for us a question about artistic
rendering that allows for odd convergences. We are led to
ask, as we take these texts seriously, whether narrative
modes of discourse can be practiced credibly in a world of

tion by Freud and Jung. The problem in the Freudian trajectory is perhaps
not so much with Freud as with those of his progeny who were excessively
"scientific" in their attention to the nature of personhood.

[7]On narrative in relation to revelation, see foundationally H. Richard
Niebuhr, *The Meaning of Revelation* (New York: Macmillan Co., 1941). Un-
fortunately, Niebuhr kept his discussion quite abstract and never dealt con-
cretely with the narratives out of which the Bible generates revelation. This
gap in his analysis has left Niebuhr open to varieties of philosophical interpretation that are considerably removed from the concreteness of narrative.
On the role of narrative in relation to the texture of social reality, see
Hayden White, *Metahistory: The Historical Imagination in Nineteenth-Cen-
tury Europe* (Baltimore: Johns Hopkins University Press, 1974).

[8]On the relation of *how* to *what* in the text, see the discussion of Gail R.
O'Day, *Revelation in the Fourth Gospel: Narrative Mode and Theological
Claim* (Philadelphia: Fortress Press, 1986).

excessive moral certitude and excessive technical control.[9] This narrative mode of rendering the world is itself subversive of technically settled social reality and is certain to be misunderstood in a society that is militantly reductionist in both religion and science.

I am, as you will see, tilting toward an argument about narrative theology.[10] I note in passing, however, that so-called narrative theology is not simply an excuse for telling interesting or clever stories. It is rather an insistence that *these are the stories.*[11] What is required of us is consummate artistry to tell these old stories as though never heard before, so that God's providence is seen as a decisive presence in the portrayal of persons, so that power is a reality reckoned with both by God and by human persons, so that self occurs in a story where God is also fully present as a character in the plot.[12] This breakthrough in Israel's faithful rendering of reality is a continuously daring alternative to our

[9]Hans Frei, in *The Eclipse of Biblical Narrative* (New Haven: Yale University Press, 1974), has traced the history of the "failure" of narrative in the epistemology of modernity. In our post-Enlightenment situation, we are now at a point of asking about a recovery of these modes of knowledge which have seemed to us naive and embarrassing. See William Placher, *Unapologetic Theology* (Louisville, Ky.: Westminster/John Knox Press, 1989), and Colin E. Gunton, *Enlightenment and Alienation: An Essay Towards a Trinitarian Theology* (Grand Rapids: Wm. B. Eerdmans Publishing Co., 1985).

[10]On narrative theology, see George W. Stroup, *The Promise of Narrative Theology: Recovering the Gospel in the Church* (Atlanta: John Knox Press, 1982).

[11]In my judgment, recent attention to canon (as in the work of Brevard S. Childs and James A. Sanders) cannot do much more than insist that "these are the stories." It cannot on the basis of that insistence also insist on a single, monopolized interpretation. Canon is a decision about the enduring significance of certain materials, but it is not a decision about a required interpretation.

[12]Ezra Pound once said that a novel is "news that stays news." My reference is from William H. Willimon, "Eyewitnesses and Ministers of the Word," *Interpretation* 42 (1988): 159–160. On seeing God "as," see Garrett Green, *Imagining God: Theology and the Religious Imagination* (San Francisco: Harper & Row, 1989), 73, 140, and passim. Green refers to "as" as the "copula of imagination."

various reductionisms, whether the reductionisms are theological and moral or are some form of social-scientific explanation of reality. I believe there are crucial implications for exegesis, for theological education, and for ministry in seeing how these stories render reality as an artistic alternative. They invite us to think alternatively to our best theology, our convinced social ideology, our favorite psychology.

From Samuel to Irangate

My pondering about this convergence of providence, power, and personality in artistic rendering has been done in the midst of the "Irangate" or Iran-contra scandal and Senate hearings regarding the sale of arms to Iran and the administration's secret channeling of funds to the Nicaraguan contras after Congress had outlawed direct military aid.

I have not explicitly pursued those issues, but no doubt my context of study has sharpened some questions for me. I have been asking, for instance: How can we make sense out of the shame and jeopardy of Irangate and yet avoid making reductionist explanations that fit our political preferences? I do not believe that the factors which made Irangate are peculiar in our common experience, but our recurring propensities are only dramatically visible there.

The notorious event of Irangate functions as a model for a number of dramatic convergences that might be cited in our common, public, historical experience. We approach such a dramatic convergence not as court reporters, to get all the facts straight, but as theological expositors, to see how an artistic rendering of the event might be shaped concerning the issues of power, providence, and personality. At the outset we come primarily with questions, the same kind of questions that must have lain behind the narrative exposition of Samuel.

Concerning *power*, one wonders about the ideological force that, while it may not be conspiratorial, has such compelling power. How strange that the ideology of heroic anti-communism is more compelling than the rule of law, and that deception is not wrong if used in a good cause. Moreover, instruments of government are easily bent to private ideological commitments and are deeply rooted in economic interest and political egoism. Such powerful ideology makes Saul's pathology, Joab's cynicism, and David's ruthlessness look modest and dull.

We dare to ask about *providence* in Irangate. Is there a hovering purpose that presides over the process in ways that our modernity does not want to credit? Is it lucky or providential that Senator Inouye's war record outshines that of Oliver North? Or is it good fortune that McFarlane has no pipe to smoke like Admiral Poindexter, but he sheds purging tears that break the facade? Or more largely, is it happenstance that President Reagan was made politically weak and yearned to have a disarmament treaty, and that the weakness he faced required him to move beyond his anti-communist ideology to care about disarmament? Could providence override power and break personality? And does that permit us to speak of a holy One who keeps watch over her own and who in the end may echo Reagan and dare to say, "Disarmament happened on my watch?"

Concerning *personality,* we can ask: How did such a Promethean battle occur between Oliver North, who embodies what is dark, doubtful, and heroic, and Daniel Inouye, who is not visibly heroic but steadfast and unintimidated, supported by Warren Rudman, who is a credentialed conservative with a decency that stops short of ideology? The flood of characters through the hearing room makes one wonder how they all happened to be there. The cast of characters who rush through the hearing room is not unlike the casting of the narrative of 1 and 2 Samuel. It is an odd company— and while we celebrate the cast, none has even asked out loud how it was so convenient for Mr. Casey to die and therefore not to testify.

Notice the provisional quality of my statements, the unanswered questions, the hiddenness that hints but does not disclose. How could one speak of all these matters except by artistic narrative that does not grind the facts too hard, that does not know too much, but that refuses cynicism? That sort of "narrative daring" is what we have all over the Bible, and especially in Samuel. These are the kinds of questions that lie behind the Samuel narrative, questions of sociology that must not be too reductionist, questions of theology that must not be too frontal, questions of psychology that must not be too analytical or romantic.

The answers to our questions and the outcome of the narrative may not be arrived at directly, but only playfully, subtly, slowly. If we are to read such artistic texts, we must read them with the same range of questions and wonderments, with the same patience and watchfulness. Such an artistic convergence of power, providence, and personality is, I propose, required if we are to make faithful sense out of Irangate or any part of our life.

The Pastoral Task

Finally I have had in mind my readers, who include pastors, would-be pastors, daring and unsettled believers, and would-be believers. We are not the kinds of folk who turn up in Senate hearings very often, nor are we called on for great public pronouncements. Except for our friendly voyeurism, no one really cares what we think of Irangate. The issues are for us much more immediate and daily: a father who has lived too long, a child caught in drug dependence, a marriage somehow gone awry, a bounced check, a low examination grade, a failed committee, a lost faith, a fresh resolve, a gift inexplicable, a dazzling act of forgiveness, anger that energizes—or destroys—the stuff of life and faith and ministry.

We are left with a slow, painful, patient, hopeful retelling, which observes while strange convergences take place, convergences that are beyond our understanding but are available for our retelling and renoticing. We are not spectators to these stories in the books of Samuel. When we yield enough, with enough patience, it becomes clear that we are in the midst of the stories—valuing our own past, pushed by ruthless force, oddly visited by the one whom we dare call God. The pastoral task is managing these stories so that they become a distanced, disclosing alternative rendering of our own life, so that the reality of power, the inscrutability of providence, and the cruciality of personhood are each permitted a say, without which we shall never see clearly, love dearly, or follow nearly.

This general perspective, of course, requires specific textual explication. In taking up a specific text, I do not imagine that the text describes. Rather, the narrator has available certain memories, facts, and traditions. The narrator makes choices (as must we) and engages strategies that converge, disclose, hide, heal, and transform. Not only does our listening hold the prospect that we shall be illuminated; indeed, each time we listen there is a chance that by this artistic rendering we shall be transformed.

2

Sport of Nature

First Samuel 18 consists of five narrative elements.[1] Three concern Saul's children, Jonathan (vs. 1–5), Merab (vs. 17–19), and Michal (vs. 20–28). There is an extended narrative about Saul and David (vs. 6–16). Finally, there is a quick theological verdict supplied by the narrator (vs. 29–30). These five pieces no doubt originally were not related to each other. The narrator takes them and builds a new narrative world for Israel. It is the world of one man, Saul, and that one man's family: Jonathan, Merab, and Michal. It is the story of one man's world disrupted. We may assume with scholars that the story is about the "Rise of David."[2] Saul, however, did not know the story was about David. He thought it was a narrative in which he was the crucial character. Saul thought that his family had gone mad, gone awry, gone out of grace, simply, cruelly, gone. Saul had to ask: What has happened to my family, my throne, my life? This narrative answers Saul's questions.

[1]In my paper "Narrative Coherence and Theological Intentionality in 1 Samuel 18" (forthcoming) I have dealt more fully with the critical and analytical issues in this text.

[2]On the narrative of "the Rise of David" and related critical matters, see Kyle McCarter, *I Samuel*, Anchor Bible (Garden City, N.Y.: Doubleday & Co., 1980), 27–30. The terms of the discussion of critical issues in current scholarship largely derive from Leonhard Rost, *The Succession to the Throne of David*, tr. David M. Gunn (Sheffield: Almond Press, 1982).

The five narrative elements are grouped together just after the defeat of Goliath by David. At the end of chapter 17, David is speaking to Saul, telling him his family connection (vs. 55–58). Chapter 18 begins abruptly with a startling dislocation.

Jonathan's Bonding

1 Samuel 18:1–5. This is Jonathan's scene. Jonathan is a key player in Saul's family. In chapter 14 Jonathan had dazzled Israel and had confounded the piety of Saul (14:45). Now the text has Jonathan focus quickly and decisively on the person of David. "When he [David] had finished speaking . . . , the life of Jonathan was knit to the life of David" (v. 1). The verb "knit" (*qšr*) can be read "be bound to," but it also means "conspire with" (22:8, 13). The narrator takes a carefully chosen ambiguous word, *qšr*, to assert a close bond between David and Jonathan that is inevitably a threat to Saul. David is to be the hero of the story, and now Saul's heir apparent is smitten with him. The word "knit" is echoed by the word "love" (*'hb*) in verse 1: "Jonathan loved David as he loved his own life." The word "love" implies both political commitment and personal affection and loyalty. The words "knit" and "love" are gathered together in verse 3: "Jonathan made a covenant with David, because he loved David as he loved his own life." We watch while Jonathan is weaned from his past loyalty to his father.[3]

This threefold claim of "knit-love-covenant" is given a sacramental embodiment by Jonathan. He strips himself and gives David his robe, his armor, his sword, his bow, his girdle—everything (18:4). Jonathan cedes to David his power, his legitimacy, his authority, his claim to the throne. What a way for David's story to begin! This "nobody" has intruded between royal father and son, and at the outset is given a provisional enthronement by Jonathan. The action between

---

[3]On "loyalty" in the David narratives and more generally, see Katherine Doob Sakenfeld, *Faithfulness in Action* (Philadelphia: Fortress Press, 1985).

David and Jonathan happens very quickly. There is no prep-
aration or explication. The action only takes four verses, and
the characters exhibit little vitality. The figures are plastic.
David is passive. Jonathan is silent. No one speaks. The narrative lets all the action happen by a few carefully chosen
verbs.

To conclude this episode, the narrator adds in 18:5:

1. "David was everywhere successful." David had a
   golden touch. He always won.
2. Saul gave him a commanding position. Even Saul liked
   David and respected him.
3. The people and the court clique approved David.

David had everyone and everything going for him. It is
amazing how quickly the claim of David could emerge, almost by itself, without anyone really taking an initiative. In
17:58 Saul does not even know the name of David. Now
everyone knows and sings and celebrates this newcomer.

Songs and Status

1 Samuel 18:6–16. The second narrative piece focuses on
tension between Saul and David, a tension about which we
have had no inkling. The two warriors are coming home
from the defeat of Goliath, Saul the successful king, David
the new, young hero. The narrator subtly anticipates the
tension between Saul and David. David returned but the
women came out to meet Saul (v. 6). Saul is still the one in
charge and the women must in the first instance greet the
king. The women may have wanted to meet David, but they
must meet Saul. Protocol requires it. The women are singing. That is what women do in ancient Israel. Since Miriam,
the women are the ones who take specific military successes
and turn them into public lore (cf. Ex. 15:20–21). The
women sing in celebration for both men, for the king and for
the hero. They sing, as Israelites almost always do, in parallel lines. They know two things about parallels. Saul has to

be mentioned first, and the second line has to intensify the first.[4]

The new song first celebrates the king:

> Saul has slain his thousands.

Then comes the second line, which unsettled Saul and anticipated the coming preeminence of David:

> David has slain his ten thousands.

There is enough joy and adulation from the women for both men. They should both have waved and smiled and been glad.

The narrator intrudes to tell us a hidden detail (18:8). No one else may have noticed, but it is the business of the narrator to notice and to cause us to notice. Saul is acutely sensitive. He celebrates this David, but then he immediately feels threatened. Saul says (we may wonder to whom; no doubt to the narrator): "What more can he have [since he already has everything]—except the throne?" (v. 8). Quickly Saul is half crazed with envy. Saul has not yet faced up to the governing promise voiced tersely in 16:12, that God wills David to have the throne. Saul in his mad jealousy has nonetheless discerned, as has no one else, that Yahweh's commitment to David is a deep threat to Saul. The text adds nicely, "He eyed David from that day forward" (v. 9). Saul spied; he looked and looked and became preoccupied. The more he watched, the more he saw what no one else could see or needed to see.

The narrative takes an enormous leap in 18:10. This is the counter story, which the narrator shares with us, but which is withheld from the characters in the story: "An evil spirit from God rushed upon Saul." The evil spirit, come to dismantle Saul, is authorized by God. It will not do to say Saul is "depressed" and reduce his problem to psychology. In his

---

[4]Robert Alter, *The Art of Biblical Poetry* (New York: Basic Books, 1985). Alter's primary thesis is that in biblical parallelism, the second line *intensifies* the first line. This is precisely the pattern the women have followed in singing of Saul and David.

pathology Saul is smitten by nothing less than the powerful, crushing reality of God, driven by a force he does not know and cannot resist. Saul goes berserk in his jealousy, his fear, and his competitiveness.

The evil spirit initiates a vicious cycle of drivenness and taming. Saul is driven by the spirit. David is summoned to tame the spirit with sweet music (18:10). Saul is soothed. Saul soothed, however, must inevitably notice his comforting musician. It is David who soothes, and the royal rage is thereby escalated, so that the music is needed the more. There is an endless spiral of rage and music. Rage wins briefly. Saul strikes out at David (v. 11). David escapes, however, because he always escapes. David is on the loose in Saul's kingdom and in Saul's family. Conversely, Saul is helpless and hopeless.

The narrator escalates the crisis for Saul. Saul is afraid of David (18:12) because the kingdom is now in jeopardy. The lyric of "thousands, ten thousands" continues to ring in Saul's ears. Indeed the song will ring in Saul's disturbed ears until he dies. Saul now imagines David wants the throne, though David has given no such hint. Saul is aware of his own futility. Saul knows now that the odds against him are enormous, even though he continues to bear the title of king. The real reason for fear, however (so the narrator proposes), is that "the Lord was with [David]" (v. 12). This is the first reference in his chapter to Yahweh. "God" (*'elohîm*) has been mentioned once before: The evil spirit is from God (v. 10). The name Yahweh, by contrast, is reserved for comment on David. The terms "God" (cf. v. 10 in relation to Saul) and "Yahweh" (cf. v. 12 in relation to David) perform different functions in the narrative. "God" is a generic name and can be on the lips of anyone. Thus the narrative carefully uses this word for Saul, subtly excluding him from contact with "Yahweh." In contrast, the name "Yahweh" used in relation to David bespeaks the Israelite tradition of covenant faithfulness. Too much should not be made of this distinction, but the two uses tilt the theological freight of the narrative decidedly in David's direction. With the mention of Yahweh, Saul is now powerfully, decisively outnumbered.

This daring, popular soldier is too visible, too close to power, too much in the public eye, too available for the media. Saul reassigns David as a field commander in a less conspicuous, certainly more dangerous place (18:13). That should have settled matters, except that this David never loses. David turns his obscure position into a public triumph (vs. 14–16). David wins and the people approve. He parades in and out, always succeeding, and the people applaud. Only the narrator knows the reason David is successful: Yahweh is with him. David has great success and Saul is in dread (v. 15). The RSV says "in awe," but the word is better read as "trembling, terrified, in dread."

The contrast between the two characters has developed sharply, quickly, irreversibly. We watch while a powerful man is reduced to putty, while a nobody without credentials takes everyone and everything by storm. The end of this second narrative element is that "all Israel and Judah loved David" (v. 16). This is the second use of "love." We have moved from Jonathan's love to Israel's love. In chapter 8, Israel had asked for a king who would go out and come in and win battles (8:20). This is he! The narrator has made the identification for us without being explicit. Saul is immobilized. He is not the real king. He cannot do what a king must do. He does not go out and come in and win battles. Power has slipped away from Saul. Power moves toward David because Israel loves him, because Yahweh is with him. There is more going on here than Saul's disturbed categories can manage. The narrator, however, does not care if Saul (or we) can explain. It is enough now to notice and be astonished.

A Desperate, Daring Offer

1 Samuel 18:17–19. Saul sees that David must be eliminated as an intolerable threat. Saul is a remarkable combination of destructive pathology and clear thinking. He is a man driven by God's evil spirit, though he does not know it. At the same time Saul knowingly chooses the disaster into which he is driven. The power of God is at work in Saul, but

Saul is still determining his own way toward David. He has thrown a spear at David. He has redeployed David. In both cases, Saul's rage has failed. Now Saul moves to a more desperate strategy, an arranged marriage. Saul will use domestic relations for political reasons. He will deploy his daughter to seduce David to his death.

Saul offers David his daughter Merab to marry (v. 17). Saul will take David as his son-in-law. The only requirement is that David fight "the battles of Yahweh." The narrator lets us know more than Saul speaks. The narrator translates the dark intent of the theological rhetoric for us. "Battles of Yahweh" is code language for fighting the Philistines. "Fighting" in the rhetoric of military leaders regularly means "getting killed." Saul's son-in-law will be duty-bound to fight the Philistines. If David faces the Philistines regularly, he is sure to be killed. Public strategies, Saul anticipates, ruthlessly serve personal ends. Saul is desperate, and therefore shameless. He will use his daughter in his powerful obsession with David.

Even this desperate ploy, however, will not work. David is characteristically proper and deferential before the king. David's propriety saves him: He is unworthy of being the king's son-in-law. He must respectfully decline Saul's offer. David acts, so we are led to believe, in innocence and is thereby saved; David's innocence is nicely contrasted to Saul's deathly cunning. Saul's strategy here is not unlike David's later disposal of Uriah (2 Samuel 11). David also was willing to use public strategies for ruthless personal ends. Even in such deathly plots, however, David can succeed while Saul characteristically fails. Saul is alone and can do nothing (cf. John 15:5).[5]

The episode has an odd turn to it. Saul does not answer

[5]David M. Gunn, *The Fate of King Saul, Journal for the Study of the Old Testament* Supp. 14 (Sheffield: JSOT Press, 1980), and W. Lee Humphreys, *The Tragic Vision and the Hebrew Tradition* (Philadelphia: Fortress Press, 1985), 23–66, have urged that Saul's story is an account of tragic fate in which Saul is helpless before a decision Yahweh has already made on behalf of David.

David's refusal. Saul does not argue with David. The narrative simply tells us that by the time of David's negative response, Saul had given his daughter to another husband (18:19). The reassignment of Merab to another husband may simply reflect historical fact. Inside the narrative, however, it may also be a measure of Saul's instability, his frantic rush from act to act without coherence. Saul is unable to sustain even his own strategy. The narrative portrays without comment the further collapse of Saul.

A Second Offer, Now Accepted

1 Samuel 18:20-28. A fourth episode reiterates the theme of vs. 17–19, the offer of a daughter in order to ensnare David. This time the daughter made available is Michal. The account begins abruptly. "Michal loved David" (v. 20). Everybody loves David! Jonathan loves David (v. 3). Israel and Judah love David (v. 16). And now Michal! Saul is clearly isolated. These are all people who should have loved Saul the most. Saul, however, is alienated from those who were his proper constituency.

Saul is said to be "delighted" at Michal's affection for David (18:20). Again we are taken by the narrator into Saul's dark thoughts. This time there is no theological code language about the "wars of Yahweh." Saul's intent is more blatant as he becomes more desperate. David must die at the hands of the Philistines (v. 21). Michal's love is useful to Saul, but it is not valued or respected by him. In his desperation, Saul's daughter's love is a tradable commodity.

The narrative becomes artfully complicated to show us the high stakes, the shamelessness of Saul, and the toughness of David. After the initial offer of Michal (18:21), there are careful negotiations carried on by court advisers. A king cannot bargain, but he can negotiate. Tell David anything to ensnare him. Tell him, "The king delights in you" (v. 22). Saul once delighted in David, but no more. Saul's delight had turned to fear and rage and hate. The narrator exposits the destructive power of rage long before Dostoevsky and

Freud had their turn in noticing the dark spoiling of the human heart. Everything is now sour for Saul. But tell David anyway. Tell him something that all parties know to be false. Tell him, secondly, in a parallel line, that the king's servants, the royal entourage, "love him." This is the fourth use of the word "love" in the chapter. This time we do not know whether to believe it. Perhaps Saul thinks he is lying about the love of his servants for David, when in fact they love David more than Saul would guess or permit.

Again David declines (18:23). David again asserts his unworthiness. He will not be used or caught. David, in regal language, regards the role of the king's son-in-law more seriously than does Saul. David speaks and thinks and acts more like a king than does Saul. He declines a second time.

This time, however, with more narrative power, Saul is insistent. Saul finally bargains, again through mediators (18:25). Saul knows how to entrap David. Appeal to David's courage, his virility, perhaps his vanity. Issue a challenge to him. The offer of a bride is not a free offer. The bride will cost and perhaps David is too much of a coward to pay. Saul's price is 100 Philistine foreskins, to be gotten only at great risk. To this kind of challenge David can relate. The offer is "right in David's eyes" (v. 26), even as Michal's love was "right in the eyes of Saul" (v. 20). There are layers and layers of duplicity here. David can hold his own with the desperate, cunning king.

David brings the required price quickly. Saul asked 100 foreskins. David brings 200 and is unscathed by the risk (v. 27). It is as though David is cherished, guarded, and protected, can do no wrong, cannot be hurt. No trouble will befall him. He will fear no evil (Ps. 23:4). He receives his wife who loved him. He becomes the king's son-in-law. Thus David intrudes into the center of Saul's family in yet another way in his relentless journey to power.

At the end of this marriage narrative, Saul finally notices two things (18:28). First, Saul sees that Yahweh is with David. Saul has not noticed that he himself is driven by God's evil spirit; but he has noticed David's well-being and has drawn the conclusion that any theologically sensitive person

would draw: Providence is operative. "Yahweh is with him."
Second, Saul notices that Michal loves David. Or is it Israel
that loves him? The text is disputed.[6] We know it is both—
Michal loves David, Israel loves David. Everyone loves David, and Saul notices. David increases in favor with God and
with humankind. The pathos of the narrative is that the matter of David's success is so clear that even Saul, in his distor-
tion, must face the emerging narrative reality. David's
secure position cannot be avoided any more than it can be
explained.

A Freighted Reprise

1 Samuel 18:29–30. Chapter 18 is a long artistic rendering
of Saul's life. Around this one song of the women about
thousands and ten thousands are gathered the terseness of
Jonathan, the passivity of Merab, the passion of Michal.
With great artistic daring, the narrator sketches out the in-
credible conflict upon which Israel's life now pivots. The
narrator has the capacity to take grand public themes and
locate them in the intimate conversations that people hold in
private. The narrative pieces available to the narrator were
originally isolated, odd memories. The narrator has, however, brought them together into a whole that is more than
the sum of the parts. On the sum of the parts now completed, a conclusion can be drawn (vs. 29–30).

Saul is more afraid (18:29). Well he might be, because he
now knows he labors against "principalities and powers,"
i.e., against both providence and personality. There is more
going on in this conflict than conversation and cunning.
There is a power at work that countermands every act and
intention of Saul and rightly generates fear. This massive
power is a power now plainly unfriendly to Saul.

---

[6]See McCarter, *I Samuel,* 320–321. The Masoretic text has "Michal
loved him," and the Septuagint has "Israel loved him." It is impossible to
adjudicate between the two readings. Either serves well the dramatic development of the narrative.

David has success (18:30). Indeed the story is precisely about David's several successes—with Jonathan, with Michal, with Israel, with the Philistines. Saul had thought the Philistines would be the death of David (v. 25). As usual, however, Saul miscalculates. The Philistine threat did not destroy David, any more than did Saul's redeployment of him. David succeeds in everything. The narrator has artfully asserted that reality, and now Saul is made to observe it.

The final line is a wondrous narrative twist. David's name is "exceedingly precious." The RSV has "highly esteemed," but the name is more than esteemed. It is treasured, cherished. But precious to whom? The narrator is silent on the point. Surely it does not betray the narrator to suggest that, in addition to Jonathan, Michal, and the people of Israel, the name is also precious to Yahweh. Yahweh also loved to say the name of David, the one after Yahweh's own heart. To Saul, however, the same precious name has a sound of deep bitterness.

What a tale! The two men had returned home together, joyous and triumphant. It took only one refrain from the women to sour Saul and to twist the course of Israel's life forever. Now Saul is forever David's sworn enemy. What Saul cannot see is that he will in the end only destroy himself, because the destiny of David will not yield to Saul's pathological rage. Saul has misread the shape and future of his own life. His anti-David policy will only isolate and finally destroy. Indeed, the isolation and destruction of Saul have already begun. This chapter, which seems like a series of fragments, is an awesome tracing of a deep fall and a treasured rise. History is not steadiness, but a series of hard, surprising breaks. By the end of the chapter, Saul is broken.

Artistic "Facts," Daring Construal

Our study of 1 Samuel 18 indicates that it is an artistic combination of diverse fragments that originally had no connection to each other. The two longer elements in vs. 6–16 on Saul and David and vs. 20–28 on Michal and David are cleverly and subtly framed articulations of David's amazing good fortune and Saul's dismal failure. The Merab episode of vs. 17–19 seems to be a modest replication of vs. 20–28. The Jonathan episode of vs. 1–5 is almost programmatic and thematic, lacking narrative specificity. The final verses of the verdict in vs. 29–30 are of course not narrative memory but *theological verdict,* a verdict derived from the narrative material. It is a verdict in which faith in Yahweh and faith in David converge.

The narrator, however, does not simply report and gather. The narrator shapes and renders to transform the material into something other than it was, something more. The narrator is relentless with the materials, not imposing on them but insisting that they yield the hidden voices that a first reading might not notice. When the hidden voices are heard, what emerges are three pervasive and uncompromising themes.

The first theme is David's success. David is "successful" in all that he does (18:5, 14, 15, 30). In three of these cases, the particular reference is to fighting battles. David is shown to be the one "who goes out and comes before Israel and wins battles." The fourth use, in v. 15, does not speak of mere military success but asserts, "Saul saw that he had great success." Saul noticed everything, but he did not want to face it. We are required, as was Saul, to recognize David's luck, prowess, and vitality.

The second theme is found in the fivefold use of the word "love" in chapter 18:

v. 1   Jonathan loved him as his own life.
v. 3   Jonathan loved him as his own life.
v. 16   All Israel and Judah loved him.
v. 20   Saul's daughter Michal loved him.
v. 28   [in the Hebrew text] Michal loved him.
        [in the Greek text] All Israel loved him.

"Love" here expresses not only personal affection and attraction but also loyal political commitment. The range of uses of this theme in this chapter stretches from the most personal, with Jonathan and Michal, to the most public, "all Israel and Judah."

The third theme pushes matters even further: "Yahweh was with him" (18:14). Such a statement is no longer reportage but is a verdict rendered by the narrator on the basis of all the narrative material of the four detailed episodes.

> Saul was afraid of David, *because the* LORD *was with him* but had departed from Saul. (v. 12)
> David had success in all his undertakings, *for the* LORD *was with him.* (v. 14)
> Saul saw and knew that *the* LORD *was with David.* (v. 28)

This last phrase, "Saul saw and knew," is parallel to 18:15. It is not enough to have David's success objectively stated. Saul, who in the process of this narrative is defeated, must be made to look the reality of David in the face. Saul is made to suffer because everything in his life has now turned against him. We are invited to enter into Saul's suffering as much as we joined the women in singing David's success. The narrator is a consummate artist because the conclusion to this tale comes, almost inevitably, from the narrative. In the end we know no other conclusion could have been drawn: Saul cannot hold the throne. It belongs to another. Saul has failed and is dismissed by the narrative.

In light of this narrative analysis I return to my three initial themes of providence, power, and personality. I do not wish to impose a particular scheme of interpretation, but these three themes do in fact emerge forcefully from the narrative.

1. The *personality of David* dominates this completed narrative. David is loved, loved, loved, and can do no wrong. David is largely passive; one cannot, however, mistake that the narrator—and Saul, Jonathan, Michal, and the women— regard David as a "sport of nature," as a mutation in social expectations, as a *novum* that cannot be understood or explained but can only be marveled at. The *Oxford English Dictionary* characterizes a "sport of nature" as "A plant. . . , animal, etc., which exhibits abnormal variation or departure from the parent stock or type . . . ; a spontaneous mutation; a new variety produced in this way." It occurs to me that in the imagination of Israel, David is precisely such a

"sport of nature," impossible to understand in terms of any already existing categories in Israel. We may compare him to Hillela in Nadine Gordimer's story *A Sport of Nature*, for each time David is almost understood in Israel, he enacts a surprising newness quite unexpected from the already known David.[7]

---

[7]The phrase "sport of nature," which is the title of this chapter, I have taken from the title of Nadine Gordimer's novel *A Sport of Nature* (New York: Alfred A. Knopf, 1987).

Behind the use of Gordimer is the much earlier use by W. E. B. Du Bois, *Black Folk Then and Now* (New York: Henry Holt & Co., 1939), 372. Du Bois uses the phrase to refer to the "unexpected" emergence of "ability" among Africans outside the monopoly and tight control of the English colonial oligarchy. He writes: "The present British oligarchy is perhaps the most remarkable in the world. It is rich and educated, and it is saved from degeneracy and inbreeding by constant recruiting of ability from all ranks of life in England, its colonies and dependencies, and even from foreign lands. This oligarchy controls democracy and limits its scope.

"A largely unexpressed but central thesis of English rule is the conviction that ability, while inherent in the English ruling class, is, outside that class, largely accidental and *a sport of nature*. This deep-seated belief assumes that present methods of education and opportunity are securing for England a fair maximum of ability, while, in all probability, it is securing a dangerous minimum and thus curtailing and killing the growth of democracy at its very source. Even in England and the white British dominions, the ability and capability of mankind have not begun to be exploited. Today it is largely accident that a Ramsay MacDonald or a Keir Hardie escape jail, asylum, or dumb obscurity. A system of broad education for children and adults, an increasing attempt to give wider and wider masses of men the same opportunity to develop strength and ability as is now reserved for the darlings of the gods and a few *sports of fate*, would in time widen the basis of democracy in England, or rather make it feasible so to broaden the limits of democratic control as to bring under its purview the whole realm of work and wage, wealth and income, production and distribution, as well as the welfare of the five hundred million persons whom Great Britain rules today chiefly for the private profit of the English ruling class. (Lack of faith in the possibilities of its people—English and white, as well as yellow, brown and black, is the danger of British Democracy.)"

It is noteworthy that Du Bois uses the phrase "sport of nature" in parallel to the phrase, "sport of fate." Both terms are used ironically if not sarcastically as a protest against the elitist assumptions of the colonial mindset. Gordimer's usage may be derived from Du Bois, but it is not applied in an explicitly pejorative way.

The narratives of David are so powerful and compelling because David is indeed a *mutation in* ancient Israel. Israel does not know what to make of him, and the narrators are constantly surprised by him. He can be explained by none of his antecedents, religious or political. He is a genuine *novum* in ancient Israel, and perhaps in narrative portrayal anywhere. When one brings a theological interest to this notion of mutation, then we may say that David is such a surprise because of the working of God's providence. There is more operative in the life and person of David than can be explained in any conventional way. That "more" is an enactment of God's hidden providence; the hiddenness requires artistic rendering to have its say.

2. There is more here than David's dazzling personality, however. There is also *the reality of power*, caught in the phrases "went out and was successful" (18:5) and "went out and came in" (v. 13). Unlike chapter 17, here David is not a lone warrior. He leads armies. Slowly the armies of Israel begin to overrun the armies of the Philistines. Much of the credit goes to David, but David does not emerge in social isolation. Social realities such as supplies, organization, technology, and public opinion are at work. These social realities are freshly mobilized around David. While we watch, Israel as a fragile, marginal people begins to assume effective and formidable power, even against the haughty Philistines. If public power had not flowed toward Israel, the David story would not be more than a hero tale of passing interest. It is, however, more than that. It is the story of how a people emerged as significant in the course of world affairs in its time and place.

3. Power and personality are clearly not the sum total of the narrative either. There is all through, in, with, and under this narrative a recognition and even an *articulation of providence*. Providence is given both positive and negative recognition. Positively, this hidden insistence is offered in the phrase "Yahweh was with him." What an odd phrase! How was God with him? What does it mean that God was with him, and how would God's presence be recognized? How would Yahweh be effective? How could it matter? Only be-

lievers know. The affirmation is a theological verdict. The credibility of the verdict is based on and derived from specific cases. Israel never concluded that "this is the messiah" until it affirmed that "the blind see, the lame walk, the dead are raised" (Luke 7:22). Israel's theological verdict lives very close to and depends on narrative specificity.

"Narrative specificity" is the way Israelite thinking and biblical theology proceed. That is, they engage in no great generalization but make the theological case one episode at a time. Thus our narrator makes no general claim for God's providence but simply shows, one text at a time, how David is strangely kept safe and brought to success. Conversely, the narrative refrains from a general theological dismissal of Saul; rather, it simply provides rich, concrete evidence that Saul's life was about to destruct, perhaps self-destruct.

The procedure of narrative specificity, so crucial to the faith claims of the Bible, is evident in two other important spheres of reflection. First, the New Testament proceeds in the same way about Jesus. While the epistles make larger claims, the gospel data behind those claims is concrete and specific. Thus, for example, in Luke 7:18–23 John poses a large question of the identity of the messiah. Jesus' response is not a general statement but a recitation of specific acts that permit and require a certain conclusion. Second, in a quite derivative sense, Sigmund Freud came to see that personal health is essentially a narrative enterprise in which the subject must reengage, one episode at a time, the sense of self that is less than functional. This narrative specificity is crucial in entering into the claims and testimony of the Bible, and specifically into the claims of the narratives we are considering. In this case, the positive affirmation of God's providence is not stated programmatically; rather, we are permitted to watch and see as the authority of that providence operates in the narratives.

Negatively, providence is acknowledged in verse 10: "An evil spirit from God rushed upon Saul." That acknowledgment also is a conclusion, not a premise. The data to support such a verdict are the cynicism, brutality, instability, and ineffectiveness of Saul. Such specific evidence leads the narrator to a conclusion concerning the reality and decisiveness of providence.

Thus the narrative is about the *person* of David who is "loved," the reality of *power* in "success," and the presence of *providence*, "for the LORD was with him." This narrative rendering of Israel's life is about all of these themes. Around these great themes, however, there also works more "daily" human reality. The narrative is in fact about a son who loves his friend more than his father, about women who sing an unwise parallelism, about a king in disarray for whom nothing works, about a daughter who loves more than her father intended, about a man who doubles the foreskin quota, and finally about a narrator who dares to fashion faith out of such details of life. The move made by the narrator from *data* to *verdict*, however, is neither necessary nor required, neither obvious nor given. It is imaginatively construed.[8] Other configurations, other hidden voices, other theological verdicts are thinkable. Thus the assemblage of Saul, his sons and daughters, the women and the crowds, and David, does not need necessarily and automatically to lead to the conclusion that "the LORD was with him." It would have been possible to draw the conclusion that Saul is either stupid or simply unlucky. It would have been plausible to talk about David's raw sexual power that drew women to him and that was a magnet for like-minded men who were ambitious and driven. It would have been credible to say that the singing of the women generated mass hysteria, or that manipulation of media created ideological power for David. The data would have permitted any of these conclusions that could have been made credible. My point is that the theological verdict was not self-evident on the surface of the narrative. It re-

---

[8]The notion of "imaginative construal" is taken from David H. Kelsey, *The Uses of Scripture in Recent Theology* (Philadelphia: Fortress Press, 1975). Kelsey, however, confines his consideration of imaginative construal to contemporary interpretation. I suggest the same imaginative construal is at work in the text itself. The data with which the narrator worked did not require this particular rendering, but the completed narrative is the work of a most imaginative construer.

quired an interpretive judgment and an artistic construal to shape the data toward this verdict, and this verdict alone. Other plausible conclusions are not offered here. What is offered is this one, in this way, with this man, by this narrator—for all time. The large themes of "personality, power, and providence" require such an artful playfulness because anything less would distort and betray.

Narrative Construal and Our Redescribed Selves

Because I recognize and take seriously the nature of these texts and the inclinations of those who are reading this book, I do not want to settle for simple exposition or hermeneutical exploration. I want also to probe the link to the practice of ministry.

Concerning 1 Samuel 18, I want to inquire about the relation of our study to *pastoral care,* to ask not only how this text is useful in pastoral care but how it might illuminate more broadly our understanding of pastoral care. I want to explore three notions suggested to me in the study of this text.

Our Narrative Selves. Pastoral care is essentially a literary, narrative enterprise of entering stories, submitting to stories, relinquishing stories, and being transformed by stories. In saying this, I mean to suggest that pastoral care is not and cannot be focused on psychological technique and analysis, as though human persons are objects to be fixed or problems to be solved. It goes without saying that pastoral care in the last two generations has made enormous gains by attending to the learnings of psychology. Now, however, we are faced with a very different issue—namely, that a narrow preoccupation with psychology has made our understanding of pastoral care too lean and has denied its proper context in the larger arena of cultural imagination. As soon as one moves from the leanness of psychology to the broadness of cultural imagination, we are pressed to literature and to narrative. Said another way, pastoral care belongs to the humanities, not to the social sciences. The imaginative, playful, pathos-

filled, liberating, reconciling power of narrative is more
powerful in the long run than analytic formulations and the-
ories. That is because transformation of personal and social
reality finally depends on the prior transformation of our
imagination.[9]

It is not often enough remembered that Freud, from
whom so much is derivative even for those who depart from
him, was a cultural critic. As Paul Ricoeur has seen most
clearly,[10] Freud shared with Marx and Nietzsche the tradition of suspicion which knows that our conventional cultural
self-understanding is a lie. Freud was not narrowly focused
on the individual person but understood the need for artful
illusions as alternative to repressive, coercive social ideolo-
gies that rob people of their human reality.[11] Repression is
not simply a psychological mechanism but is a large social
habit related not narrowly to sexuality but to a host of productive, consumptive operations.[12] Thus Freud's generative
and imaginative power appeals to narratives that run from
Oedipus to Narcissus with a nod to Sisyphus for us overly
labored Protestants. Freud understood that these great narratives mirror, legitimate, and invite us to self-perception.

[9]On imagination as the inscrutable, holistic route to faith, see John Henry
Newman, *An Essay in Aid of a Grammar of Assent* (1870; reprint, Notre
Dame, Ind.: University of Notre Dame Press, 1979), and derivatively, John
Coulson, *Religion and Imagination* (Oxford: Clarendon Press, 1981). See
the splendid discussion of Garrett Green, *Imagining God: Theology and the
Religious Imagination* (San Francisco: Harper & Row, 1989). Green's discussion will be enormously important and represents a significant advance
in our understanding of the role of imagination in the emergence of newness as a religious act.

[10]Paul Ricoeur, *Freud and Philosophy: An Essay on Interpretation* (New
Haven: Yale University Press, 1970).

[11]On the powerful positive importance of "illusion," see Paul W. Pruy-
ser, *The Play of the Imagination: Towards a Psychoanalysis of Culture* (New
York: International Universities Press, 1983).

[12]On the peculiar repressiveness of Jewishness in Western bourgeois culture, see John M. Cuddihy, *The Ordeal of Civility: Freud, Marx, Lévi-Strauss
and the Jewish Struggle with Modernity* (New York: Basic Books, 1974). See
also Norbert Elias, *The Civilizing Process*, vol. 2: *Power and Civility* (New
York: Pantheon Books, 1982).

Indeed, without attending to the classic narratives, we shall not understand the cultural range of health and pathology available to us.[13]

The recent history of pastoral care and pastoral counseling has of necessity paid attention to psychology, because of a need to get breathing space from heavy theological authority.[14] That move needed to be made and has been decisively made. Now we are at a very different crisis: we are facing a move away from psychological analysis to narrative transformation. Charles Gerkin has scored the point most effectively, but he simply reflects a larger move.[15] We are relational creatures; stories that shape us are narrative transactions that have enduring power.[16] Gerkin is helpful in see-

[13]Bruno Bettelheim, *The Uses of Enchantment: The Meaning and Importance of Fairy Tales* (New York: Random House, Vintage Books, 1977), has shown how "fairy tales" are essential to the health of a child, and how the lack of them stultifies imagination and contributes to unhealth. What fairy tales do for children is done, mutatis mutandis, by the "classic narratives" for adults. We need not be precise about what is "classic," but see the general discussion of David Tracy, *The Analogical Imagination* (New York: Crossroad Publishing Co., 1981).

[14]Thomas C. Oden, *Care of Souls in the Classic Tradition* (Philadelphia: Fortress Press, 1984), has traced this remarkable and sudden development in pastoral care by paying attention to the shifted references in the literature of pastoral care. Oden views this move away from classic theological references to modern psychology as a negative move. So do I, but I judge it to have been a necessary move in that particular cultural context.

[15]Charles V. Gerkin, *Widening the Horizons: Pastoral Responses to a Fragmented Society* (Philadelphia: Westminister Press, 1986). Gerkin's earlier book *The Living Human Document: Re-visioning Pastoral Counseling in a Hermeneutical Mode* (Nashville: Abingdon Press, 1984) interestingly moves in the direction of "document." I think, however, that Gerkin has not yet clarified the *textual* character of a human person. On the textual character of the self, see Richard Harvey Brown, *Society as Text: Essays on Rhetoric, Reason, and Reality* (Chicago: University of Chicago Press, 1987), 60–63, 143–171, and passim.

[16]It seems likely that "Object-Relations Theory" provides the best interface in personality theory to the theological categories of covenant, as they are characterized in narrative transactions. On the literature of "Object-Relations Theory," see Gerkin, *The Living Human Document*, pp. 81–96. On narrative dimensions of therapy, see James Hillman, "The Fiction of Case History: A Round," in *Religion as Story*, ed. James B. Wiggins (Lan-

ing how *my story* and *our story* relate to the *classical stories.*
Conversely, feminists are attentive to how classical stories
can be imperialistic and oppressive and need to be recast in
terms of "my story" and "our story." We are in the process
of telling our story and indeed in composing our story. We
rarely make a new story but give our particular casting to a
story there long before us and there long after us.

The classical Freudian stories and the more immediate
stories of health and unhealth in our common repertoire are
powerfully available to us. My purpose in this exercise, however, is to suggest that in the church (and thus in the pastoral office), the scriptures provide us with a resource of
stories that are like the other stories and also very different.
What is very different in these stories is the insistent power
of Yahweh, who creates and destroys. Yahweh is an accepted, legitimate, recognized, taken-for-granted character
in the biblical narrative. Yahweh's cruciality makes Israel's
stories odd, different, and immensely important. The classic
Greek myths that informed Freud would not allow for such a
transformative figure at their center. Nor is this transformative agent present in most of the stories we conventionally
tell each other. Most of these stories are flattened into psychological transactions without robust social reality or dangerous theological force.

The narrative perspective of the pastoral office does not
focus on Greek myths, which lack an intruding agent who
can transform. Nor does the pastoral office linger excessively
over privatized narratives, which focus on the significance of
personality and the reality of power. The pastoral office goes

ham, Md.: University Press of America, 1975), 123–173. Two comments
from Hillman bear on our study: "The idea that there is a God in our
tellings and that this God shapes the words into the very syntax of a genre is
not new in literary studies even if it might come as a shock to my colleagues
who believe they are really only writing clinical accounts of facts" (145).

"The way we imagine our lives is the way we are going to go on living
our lives. For the manner in which we tell ourselves about what is going on
is the genre through which events become experiences. There are no bare
events, plain facts, simple data—or rather this too is an archetypal fantasy"
(146).

further and reckons with an active transformative providence, a subject who is an awesome character in the midst of
our most treasured stories. It is clear, I trust, that I am not
urging a silly or irresponsible supernaturalism. I have the
impression, however, that our "health stories" have left out
the main character, and that is like narrating our unhealth
while maintaining silence about a psychotic father or a seductive mother. All the characters in the narrative must be
permitted their parts.[17] What we know in the narratives like
1 Samuel 18 is that there is more than "success" and "love."
There is also "Yahweh was with him."

Pastoral care, then, consists not in simply valuing stories
that we tell. It is attentiveness to *another story* that is our
story, a story about a hidden insistence that changes all the
other characters in the plot. Sociological and psychological
analysis, important as they are, are not adequate ways to tell
our truth.

Narrative Conclusions Beyond Necessity. The narrative of
this chapter is made up of concrete particularities. In the
end, however, the story is more than the sum of the parts.
The story consists in small actions concerning Jonathan,
Michal, Merab, and Saul. Historical criticism has been skill-
ful and attentive in analyzing the parts. In 1 Samuel 18,
however, we will understand nothing if we focus only on the
parts. Real understanding and fresh discernment require a
larger reading, an over-reading that is not automatically derived from the parts. That larger reading is a theological
verdict which can be made only playfully, tentatively, dar-
ingly. The verdict follows from the data, but it does not follow automatically. It follows only for those who have
attended to all the characters in the plot and who dare an
interpretive leap. The leap is a theological leap, informed by

[17]On the capacity to have many "characters" in the narrative, see Ste-
phen Crites, "Angels We Have Heard," in Wiggins, ed., *Religion as Story*,
23–63. Crites shows how angels can figure as significant and credible characters only in a certain kind of narrative and are necessarily and in principle
excluded from other kinds of stories.

and attentive to personality and power, but finally not embarrassed by providence. The leap of verdict made in 1 Samuel 18 is that "Yahweh was with him." The narrator, the one managing our pastoral care here, is prepared for such a leap, knows the language and the references, but waits to see if the data will permit and require such a conclusion.

Pastoral care in such a narrative context is an artistic construal of how the parts interrelate. It is not heavy-handed theology. It is not arrogant supernaturalism. It is nonetheless grounded in a recognition that there is one more character in our life story than our modernity concedes.

I know of course that there is much pathological religion, so that religion becomes dangerous in the pursuit of healing. We reckon also, however, with pathological despair and pathological subjectivism and reductionism. The theological verdict given in the narrative is not in a vacuum but takes place in a community where liturgically and educationally the decisive character of Yahweh is relentlessly, persistently, and candidly sketched out. When the verdict is given, "The Lord was with him," the listeners already have some notion of who this one is, having traced his presence from Exodus to Joshua. As we listen to the account of this character once again, the God of the great stories comes to be present in "my story" and may become the glue for the parts.

Our Stories Always Retold Beyond Us. This playful account of David and Yahweh in 1 Samuel 18 is useful for pastoral care because it *is* and it *is not* my story. It is about me and it is not about me. Bruno Bettelheim has well understood that the fairy tale shapes and authorizes the imagination of the child, creating for the child an alternative possibility.[18] Moreover, adult telling of the stories legitimates the child's engagement in imaginative exploration.

---

[18]Bettelheim, *The Uses of Enchantment,* 28 and passim. See the same point made in a different way by George Steiner, *Real Presences: Is There Anything in What We Say?* (London: Faber & Faber, 1989), 191: "If the child is left empty of texts, in the fullest sense of that term, he will suffer an early death of the heart and of the imagination.

I submit that taken seriously, taken playfully, and sensitively rendered, narratives like the one in 1 Samuel 18 provide playful opportunity for redescribing and reconstructing life. We are indeed reconstructing and retelling ourselves as we go along. It matters, therefore, what materials we have available for that reconstruction and that retelling.

As Bettelheim has shown, no child finally confuses Jack, or the Three Little Pigs, or Sinbad, or Little Red Riding Hood with herself or himself—and yet there is a wondrous participation in the plot with the other characters. So also in 1 Samuel 18, no listener now or in ancient Israel would confuse himself or herself with David. We do not do that with biblical stories. Yet it takes no great imagination, while considering Saul or David, to find our life peopled with Jonathan and Merab and Michal and singing women and ruthless spears and applauding crowds. We draw very close to the narrative and we participate. When we do draw close, criticism is overcome and the text narrates for us another world, a world in which love is possible and hatred goes crazy, in which success is rampant and the king fails, in which Yahweh is present in transformative ways. David's world is rich with people. In our *retelling* of David's story and David's world, "our story" is *repeopled.*

The narrator is not picky about our listening. He does not require us to be believers before we listen to the story. She asks modestly only that we let all the characters be present in the story. Over time we cannot help but wonder if our story is like this one.

These three points, then, are suggested to me at the interface of narrative, text, and pastoral care:

1. Narrative imagination as a context for *reimaging life*
2. A sense of *construed wholeness* comprehending all the parts
3. A story that *is our story,* and *is not our story*

We now require a handling of the biblical text that honors criticism but moves beyond criticism to an engagement with the claim of the narrative itself. It is our reduction of the Bible, our embarrassment about its innocence, our reluctance about its insistent cunning, that evokes silly religion and sillier criticism.

When these stories are absent from our experience, everything is likely to be "explained." But then noticing is not possible: thrones are never risked, songs are never sung, swords are never thrown, foreskins are never acquired, names are never precious. When everything is "explained," life is denied and no new life is imaginable. As an alternative to our "explained" lives, we are offered these stories, which break open our flattened, one-dimensional life. We think we have known the outcome of these stories for a long time. Those stories, however, now await a new, surprising retelling, for the sake of our life. When they are not retold, we must settle for things as they were. When the stories are well retold, we are offered a new world in which God's providential care outruns both our remarkable personalities and our cunning, devastating power.[19]

[19]I am glad to acknowledge the inestimable help Gail R. O'Day has given me in this chapter, as in much else of my research and writing. On this chapter, she helped me see the mapping of David's life in this narrative. Beyond that, however, she has taught me much of what I know about literary analysis and about the theological discernment that goes with such analysis. In her book *Revelation in the Fourth Gospel: Narrative Mode and Theological Claim* (Philadelphia: Fortress Press, 1986) and in her patient counsel and discernment over time, she has permitted me to read the texts more carefully, more adequately, and more knowingly. I am greatly in her debt.

3

The Seduction of Violence: Bloodguilt Avoided and Denied

Human life is a strange tale of securing power, having power, and losing power. The reality, risk, seduction, and cruciality of power outrun our capacity to understand or explicate it. Marx is undoubtedly correct in his judgment that, pushed to its origin, every concentration of power and wealth is based in some kind of seizure by violence.[1] The theme of power rooted in violence is pervasively evident in the contemporary world. As sexism and racism are exposed, and as disadvantaged peoples no longer accept conventional inequities, the connection between power and violence is starkly evident.[2]

This connection, on which so much of our common life is based, is so embarrassing and dangerous to established interests that it is difficult to find speech adequate for the reality. If, however, we are ever to tame, limit, or transform the bru-

[1]José Miranda, *Marx and the Bible* (Maryknoll, N.Y.: Orbis Books, 1974), chapter 1, has provided a clear statement of Marx's argument and has applied it especially to problems of economics.

[2]On the interface of violence and power, and on the way that speech counters violence, see the awesome statement by Elaine Scarry, *The Body in Pain* (New York: Oxford University Press, 1985), and see Susan Jacoby, *Wild Justice: The Evolution of Revenge* (San Francisco: Harper & Row, 1983). The work of René Girard has been especially important for recent scripture study on the theme of violence and religion. See Andrew J. McKenna, ed., *René Girard and Biblical Studies, Semeia* 33 (1985).

tality that lives in the midst of all our power arrangements, we must speak with candor about the linkage of power and violence. It is of course an unresolved issue whether violence that is definitional and elemental can ever be tamed; perhaps Marx is right in saying that it cannot. Great art, as in these narratives, continues to watch and hope and occasionally conjure a more excellent way. As we shall see, this narrative keeps watch over David at the break of violence. The church has mostly fled from those hard issues and has settled for more benign preoccupations. In the face of such reluctance, however, we may notice that the Bible is willing and required to speak on the subject and does so without embarrassment.

Rhetoric in the Midst of Violence

In this chapter, I take up a part of the David narrative as an example of one way in which the Bible speaks about power and violence. The David narrative is an artistic meditation on the reality of power. At the outset of the account that leads to David, Hannah sings about the one who "makes poor and makes rich," who "brings low and exalts" (1 Sam. 2:7). In this programmatic song, Hannah (and Israel) acknowledge the prospect that Yahweh may and does abruptly transform the social reality of power. As the song is now placed, Hannah sings from her experience of Samuel's surprising birth. Birth becomes in Israel the quintessential way in which God works a newness that redistributes power and transforms society. (In the Christian tradition, this attentiveness to birth as newness from God comes to fruition at Bethlehem.) This poem introduces the amazement of Hannah (Israel) at the birth of the boy Samuel. Her singing, however, moves beyond the new baby to the political horizon of Israel's kingship (1 Sam. 2:10b):

> The LORD will judge the ends of the earth;
>   he will give strength to his king,
> and exalt the power of his anointed.

As Brevard Childs and Robert Gordon have noted, the

Song of Hannah is both articulated and placed so that its intent goes well beyond the birth of Samuel to the David story which is to follow.[3] David becomes the exemplar of the poor one who is made rich, the low one who is exalted. David is presented as one who begins powerless, without claim or credential. He is the eighth son of Jesse (1 Sam. 16:10–11).

The subsequent narrative revolves around the awareness and affirmation that David will not be denied power. He goes from strength to strength. By the end of his story in 1 Kings 2:5–9, David sounds like a very old "Godfather" giving his son advice. That fatherly advice concerns how to keep and consolidate power, how to settle scores, remember, and avenge. David is now wise, jaded, and cynical, no longer the handsome figure of young innocence (cf. 1 Sam. 16:12). David turns out to be the one about whom Hannah sang. The God of her song turns out to be the God who guarantees and supports David.

The story of David is a study of how this young "nobody" becomes this cynical old man. In the middle of the story, in the narrative of "the Rise of David,"[4] we are midway between the expectations of Hannah (1 Sam. 2:1–10) and David's cynical advice to Solomon (1 Kings 2:5–9). In the narrative between these two passages, David is on the rise. He will have power. The entire narrative is bent in that direction. The narrative knows that because David is destined to power, he lives at the edge of violence. The working out of David's destiny carries with it either violence, the temptation to violence, or the appearance of violence. How else will David get to be king? As with every person who has power, Saul is not disposed to yield his throne easily to David and walk away quietly beaten. David will have to take

---

[3]Brevard S. Childs, *Introduction to the Old Testament as Scripture* (Philadelphia: Fortress Press, 1979), 272–273; Robert P. Gordon, *1 & 2 Samuel*, Old Testament Guides (Sheffield: JSOT Press, 1984), 25–26.

[4]On the critical issues and the scholarly labeling of the text, see P. Kyle McCarter, *I Samuel*, Anchor Bible, (Garden City, N.Y.: Doubleday & Co., 1980), 27–30.

the throne, but such a taking is characteristically an act of desperate, savage power.[5]

All through the story of his "rise," David lives at the brink of violence and killing. The temptation to power via violence creates for David a problem of bloodguilt, punishment, and vengeance. David, therefore, has an urgent need for acquittal from all these implied or assumed affronts. David's problem is either a problem of theological substance, for he has offended God (cf. 2 Sam. 12:7–12), or it is one of public relations. He has offended Israel's sensitivities and jeopardized his political support (2 Sam. 16:7–8). Either way, David has a problem that endangers his power and his future throne. Because of our benign interpretive preoccupations in the church wherein we look for privatistic reassurance and personal enrichment, our usual romantic readings of the story have screened out the pervasiveness of violence in these stories. If we read carefully, however, we can notice that the story has an alert, unembarrassed edge to it concerning power and violence, and an outcome of guilt. The narrative is a consummate artistic expression that deals with the weighty problems of guilt and innocence, vengeance and acquittal, addressing them with concreteness and specificity, with perceptiveness and delicacy.

Bloodguilt Avoided

In this discussion I will consider two clusters of material from the narrative of the "Rise of David." In both cases, it is evident that the theme of power and violence is very much the preoccupation of the narrator. Indeed, the narrative seems preoccupied with the question of how David comes to power, how the threat of violence hovers around the story, and how the God of Israel is shown to be at work in the midst of that threat in order to bring David to power. The first cluster consists in three consecutive stories in 1 Samuel

---

[5]Notice that in 1 Sam. 8:11–18, the central characterization of the coming monarchy is that it is a "taking" institution.

24–26. In this cluster chapters 24 and 26 are parallel accounts of the same plot. Chapter 25 stands between them, but likewise concerns the theme of power and violence.[6]

The One More Righteous: 1 Samuel 24. Here Saul once again pursues David (compare his action in 18:17, 21; 19:10, 11; 20:31; 23:13–14, 22–29). Saul stops to go into a cave to defecate. As luck (or providence) would have it, David and his men are back deep in the same cave, their presence unknown to Saul (v. 3). David's men also needed a rest stop. Because of the odd circumstance of their meeting, the roles of Saul and David are dramatically reversed. The king is now the vulnerable, exposed one, and David becomes the one in a position of power and advantage. In this dramatic narrative the hunter becomes the hunted. David now has his chance against Saul. David is tempted by his own loyal men to eliminate Saul (v. 4). David comes within a whisker of yielding to their temptation. David could have killed Saul easily and safely, and pleaded self-defense, but he does not. Instead, David "cuts off" the skirt of Saul's robe, an act symbolic of violence whereby Saul is stripped of his virility and authority.

The use of the verb "cut off" (*krt*) is freighted and crucial for the narrative. Already in 20:14–17, David has sworn to Jonathan that he will not "cut off" the house of Saul. There the verb is used three times. The use of the term focuses a crucial issue of the large narrative, namely the precariousness of Saul's house. Now, in our passage, the verb is used again. David Gunn has suggested that David's action in cutting off Saul's "skirt" is a playful allusion, not missed by Israel's listeners, to the cutting off of Saul's genitals, thus robbing Saul of his power and his future.[7] The use of the same verb with the house and name of Saul, with Saul's "skirt," and perhaps with an allusion to Saul's genitals, indi-

[6]See R. P. Gordon, "David's Rise and Saul's Demise: Narrative Analogy in I Samuel 24–26," *Tyndale Bulletin* 31 (1980): 37–67.

[7]David M. Gunn, *The Fate of King Saul, Journal for the Study of the Old Testament* Supp. 14 (Sheffield: JSOT Press, 1980), 93–95.

cates how precarious is Saul's situation in the face of David. The entire narrative is a watching and waiting to see how and when Saul's kingdom will be "cut off." It is clear that his rule cannot persist in the face of David's destiny, as crafted in this narrative.

In his act of symbolic violence against Saul, David is smitten in his heart (24:5). David is, after all, a man after God's own heart (13:14; 28:17). One would not expect such a one to have a heart murderous enough to destroy the legitimate king. It is as though David "comes to himself" (cf. 2 Sam. 24:10; Luke 15:17). David is remorseful and regretful for what he might have done and almost did to Saul. Perhaps David's cutting off the robe is a stratagem against his own men, as he talked them out of going further in doing damage to Saul (v. 7). David is close to incurring bloodguilt. He draws the line, however, against his own inclination and against the urging of his men, with the acknowledgment that Saul is "the Lord's anointed."

David dreams of power; his dream, however, has limits beyond which he will not go. In that moment of refusal, David seems to know that violence against Saul would destroy him as well as Saul. The narrator presents the temptation of David and the baseline of resistance to that temptation by which he maintained his innocence.

The remainder of the chapter consists in two long speeches. David speaks first (24:8–15). He addresses Saul with a proper title, "My lord the king" (v. 8). David bows down before Saul and proclaims his own innocence: "The Lord gave you today into my hand . . . , but I spared you" (v. 10). (Notice how Yahweh is an easily accepted character in the story.) I am innocent, I could have killed you, but I did not. Then David's tone of address changes. His voice is intimate, not regal, as he calls Saul, "my father" (v. 11). "I cut off the skirt of your robe, but I did not kill you." There sounds again that ominous word, "cut off." Having said that much, David concludes, "I have not sinned" (v. 11). David asserts his own innocence. Indeed the narrative is concerned to assert his innocence in a context where bloodguilt was a powerful temptation.

David submits himself to Saul and asks for a royal verdict. Trusting in his own innocence, after addressing Saul as "My lord the king" (24:8), he calls him "my father" (v. 11). Saul responds to David with a comparable address of intimacy: "My son David" (v. 16). Saul's voice echoes the pathos of old, troubled Isaac (cf. Gen. 27:18). Saul had been frantically hunting David in order to kill him. Now in a moment of lucidity and sanity, he calls David "my son."

And Saul weeps (24:16). Saul weeps for what could have been and will never be. Saul weeps also for what in fact will be. Saul weeps because he knows that his future is all behind him, and that the coming future belongs to David and not to him. He weeps because he has wasted his future in a fearful, squandering hatred. Saul's weeping is a pitiful coming to terms with a future that excludes him, with an acknowledgment of the hard reality of David's destiny which he did not want to acknowledge. When Saul has wept, he makes his speech of response to David.

"You are more righteous than I; for you have repaid me good, whereas I have repaid you evil" (24:17). The king's response to David is cast in juridical language. This is not the language of personal gratitude or of intimate feeling; it is entry into the ongoing public struggle of violence, power, guilt, and vengeance. The enunciation of these issues of political reality in the narrative raises questions about the possibility of forgiveness and the breaking of the cycle of fear and vengeance. The vicious cycle between the hunter and the hunted can only be broken by an act of unexpected generosity. In David's action, it is clear that forgiveness is not simply a religious matter of grace, or a human matter of gentleness and intimacy. Forgiveness is a daring political act that can reorient political conflict.[8] Because David can undertake such an act of forgiveness, a new transaction between Saul and David is made possible.

Saul's first statement in response to David is descriptive

---

[8]On the public, political dimension of forgiveness, see Carter Heyward et al., *Revolutionary Forgiveness: Feminist Reflections on Nicaragua* (Maryknoll, N.Y.: Orbis Books, 1987).

(24:17–19a). David is indeed "righteous." David has not retaliated or taken vengeance as he well might have. David is an innocent man. This descriptive statement becomes the basis for Saul's second statement, a wish that may indeed be a prayer: "May the LORD reward you with good" (v. 19). David should receive from Yahweh what he has not properly received from Saul. Saul (and David) live in a morally coherent world where this righteous man should receive a proper response for his disciplined right living. His right living has avoided bloodguilt; he has not taken vengeance upon Saul.

After the description (24:17–19a) and the wish (v. 19), the third element in Saul's speech is a dynastic promise: "And now [*we'attah*], behold, I know." Saul speaks the decisive concession: "I know that you shall surely be king and that the kingdom of Israel shall be established in your hand" (v. 20). The verb "be king" is emphatic, constructed with an infinitive absolute. At last Saul knows. Indeed, Saul is the last one to know (cf. 23:17). The narrative has let us know for a long time that David would be king. It does not count for much, however, that we know, unless and until Saul knows. Saul is the one who has to know. At this moment of Saul's admission, the terrible contest for power is over. David has come to power, without falling prey to the perpetration of vengeance and violence.

In the last element in his speech, Saul evokes from David a personal pledge that David will not destroy Saul's heirs or Saul's name (24:21). David swears (v. 22). The report of David's oath is terse; that oath nonetheless is crucial for what is to follow, for David is indeed a man of his word.

The exchange between David and Saul is a carefully crafted statement about the risk and reality of political power. David's speech to Saul asserts his innocence. He acknowledges that there is a vengeance at work. It is, however, the work of Yahweh, not of David (v. 12). David's speech presents a challenge to Saul to reperceive the dynamics between the two men in the light of Yahweh's rule. Saul's pathos-filled response to David is an acknowledgment that David's reading of reality is a correct one. Saul is put in the wrong, which leads him to concede everything to David.

In the end, Saul evokes from David only an oath for the survival of his family line. That oath, however, yields nothing for Saul's power and throne, which are now lost and conceded. David may in fact have been close to bloodguilt in his "cutting" of the robe of Saul. His speech and the response of Saul, however, make it clear that while David may live close to guilt, he is indeed innocent.

The One Who Will Do Many Things: 1 Samuel 26. The parallel account in chapter 26 follows the same story line as in chapter 24, but the narrative is more complex in its telling. Again, Saul begins as the hunter but becomes the hunted (26:5). With the ruthless Abishai, David enters Saul's camp at night (v. 7). We are not told why they have gone there, but Abishai assumes it is for a killing, for Saul is indeed David's sworn enemy. The narrative is careful to show that the enmity is on Saul's side, not David's. It is Saul who has sworn an oath to kill, not David. David's response to Abishai and his rebuke of Abishai's plea expresses the theological intention of the narrative (vs. 9–11):

> Do not destroy him; for who can put forth his hand against the LORD's anointed, and be guiltless? . . . As the LORD lives, the LORD will smite him; or his day shall come to die; or he shall go down into battle and perish. The LORD forbid that I should put forth my hand against the LORD's anointed.

Then David took Saul's spear and the water jug. As for Saul and Abner, the narrator adds: "A deep sleep from the LORD had fallen upon them" (v. 12).

Power and violence hover around this narrative. Ruthless power is embodied in the person of Abishai.[9] Along with power and violence, however, this narrative is freighted with divine providence. Six times in 26:9–12 the name of Yahweh is invoked. Some invocations of the name are merely conventions, but two are decisive for the narrative.

---

[9]On Abishai in a similar role in 2 Sam. 16:5–14, see Walter Brueggemann, "On Coping with Curses: A Study of II Samuel 16:5–14," *Catholic Biblical Quarterly* 36 (1974): 175–192.

First, "Yahweh sent a deep sleep," making Saul vulnerable for transformation (v. 12).[10] The deep sleep sent by Yahweh gives David the upper hand against Saul. Second, "Yahweh will smite him," or he will die a natural death, or he will die in battle (v. 10). Three ways are named in which Saul may die (cf. 2 Sam. 24:11–13, where David is given three options). Only the first of these is explicitly credited to Yahweh. The other two alternatives, however, also by inference, fall under Yahweh's governance. All three ways, moreover, leave David free and unimplicated by Saul's coming death. David does not doubt that the tide of history, presided over by Yahweh, pushes toward his own success. David is content not to coerce God's future but to let it work its own way. David is not only a master of cunning but a man of deep faith.

An additional element in this narrative (in contrast to chapter 24) is the taunting of Abner by David, suggesting that Abner has not kept faithful watch over Saul (26:15–16). Because of "Yahweh's sleep," we know that Abner struggles with more than flesh and blood. Abner indeed did not keep faithful watch over Saul, and his carelessness put Saul at risk. The reason for Abner's failure, however, unknown to Abner but known to us, is that the sleep is the work of Yahweh. It is sleep generated by Yahweh to protect David and to defeat Saul. Abner had no chance against the power of sleep, authorized by Yahweh. The "deep sleep" that makes the drama possible is an entry of providential power into the narrative. More is at work here than simply the human actors. The plot thickens with this entry of inscrutability.

The Abner verses only delay the primary exchange of the narrative. As in chapter 24, Saul and David confront each other, a meeting between what has been and what will be. Again it is "my son" as in 24:16 (26:17). But David's answer

[10]See Thomas H. McAlpine, *Sleep, Divine and Human, in the Old Testament, Journal for the Study of the Old Testament* Supp. 38 (Sheffield: JSOT Press, 1986). On the numinous sleep imposed on human persons by Yahweh in order that Yahweh may work a transformative or saving act, see Gen. 2:21; 15:12.

is not "my father" as in 24:11. Now David's response is formal: "My lord, O king" (26:17 as in 24:8).

After Saul's initial halting inquiry (26:17), David is permitted the first extended speech (vs. 18–20). Saul has hunted David down like a common criminal. In two challenging questions, David asserts his own innocence. David asks, "What have I done? What guilt is on my hands?" (v. 18) Then David draws a finer distinction. He wants to probe the motivation of Saul. Saul may be motivated in his hostility to David either by Yahweh or by human advisers. David believes he can counter either motivation. If it is God who powers Saul's assault against David, David will come to terms with God through an offering. It is not on the horizon of David's speech whether Saul would keep the throne if David appeased God. The speech concerns only the urgent question of David's survival and well-being. David does not doubt that his offering to God will be acceptable and effective. Perhaps David's reference to God as the instigator is a ploy. Or perhaps neither David nor the narrator are quite certain where God is operative in this exchange. If, however, Saul's hostility has a human motivation, e.g., the aggressiveness of Abner, then that destructive power behind Saul is condemned and cursed.

David's reasoning subtly indicts Saul, although David does not explicitly apply his charge to Saul. He ostensibly aims his curse not at Saul, but at Saul's advisers. The charge however surely applies to Saul as well as to his advisers. The charge is that the pursuit of David drives David out of Israel and therefore to a place away from Yahweh's realm where he must serve other gods (26:19). Saul is guilty of making David into a practicing idolater. The purpose of the speech is to put Saul in the wrong. There is in fact no serious notion that Saul's pursuit is motivated by Yahweh; that option is stated but not pursued. Nor there is any serious thought that other human agents besides Saul are responsible. It is all Saul, and Saul is wrong. Saul is wrong, and David is innocent. David's artful speech ends with a direct indictment of Saul as one who "has come out to seek my life" (v. 20).

Saul's answer concedes David's charge: "I have done

wrong" (26:21; cf. 2 Sam. 12:13). Saul's offense, so the narrator insists, is flat and obvious. Saul's condemnation is
placed in Saul's own mouth. Saul answers David's threefold
question of 18. David has no guilt. David skillfully turns
Saul's admission of guilt to his own advantage, for he is
shown to be innocent. David submits that he himself is eligi-
ble for a good reward from Yahweh. Yahweh "rewards (*šûb*)
every man in his righteousness and his faithfulness" (v. 23).
David has been righteous and faithful and should receive in
kind from Yahweh. In that one verse David invokes Yahweh's name three times: "Yahweh rewards . . . Yahweh
gave you into my hand. . . . I would not touch Yahweh's
anointed." David's petition asks nothing of Saul, for Saul has
nothing to give that David wants or needs. David asks instead that his life be precious in the eyes of Yahweh (v. 24).
That is all that counts now for David. Saul has become for
David an irrelevance.

Saul's final affirmative response to David is anticlimactic.
"Blessed be you, my son David!" The key concession has
already been made, however. Saul only acknowledges what
the preceding exchange has established. Saul's time for being taken seriously is over.[11] "You will do many things and
will succeed in them" (26:25). Through this one-on-one exchange, power has been transferred. David is vindicated.
Saul yields the future to David. The transfer of power and
legitimacy is accomplished by this dramatic exchange. The
narrator invites Israel to ponder how it is that power has
shifted, seemingly by itself, surely by Yahweh's hidden intention, without David lifting a finger.

The One Kept from Bloodguilt: 1 Samuel 25. Between the
parallel episodes of chapters 24 and 26 stands the Nabal-

---

[11]The dramatic power of Saul's acknowledgment of David is underscored
by the fact that Saul does not again speak to David. Indeed, Saul now dis-
appears from the narrative, except for the surreptitious consultation of
28:3–25 with the dead Samuel. This is Saul's last appearance as a serious
character in the story of David's rise to power. His final statement is for that
reason all the more important. His last word is legitimation of David.

Abigail narrative of chapter 25. Here David is cast, ostensibly, in a role different from that in the other two chapters. In this narrative David is the leader of a raiding band; he wants Nabal to pay him protection money (25:8). Nabal haughtily (and unwisely, as it turns out) refuses (vs. 10–11). David's response to Nabal's refusal is vigorous and violent (vs. 12–13). David is prepared to kill. He will kill all males in Nabal's defiant household.

The story is transformed from a raw, brutal confrontation to yet another anticipation of David's throne by the intervention of Abigail. She is as "discreet and beautiful" as Nabal is "churlish and ill-behaved" (v. 3). Abigail knows exactly how to appear, how to act, what to say in order to tame the rage of David. She bows before David (v. 23). She shrewdly asks that Nabal and his defiant behavior be overlooked, and that she, Abigail, be reckoned with as the voice of real authority on the farm (v. 25). She skillfully pushes her dangerous husband to the back of the stage.

In 25:26–31 Abigail makes a stunning, cunning speech with all the right ingredients. She observes that "The LORD has restrained you from bloodguilt and from taking vengeance" (v. 26), the very undertakings that David had pledged (v. 22). Abigail affirms that "Yahweh restrained" David. Abigail nicely refuses to observe that Yahweh's restraint is in fact her own effective persuasion. Abigail's intervention is what held David in check, but the narrator has shrewdly identified Abigail with Yahweh's watchful care of David. In the narrator's playfulness, we may conclude that Yahweh's providential care is nothing more than Abigail's shrewdness. Yet the speech of Abigail refutes this. More is going on here than the intervention of a clever woman. This hidden providence is indeed hidden in Abigail. It cannot, however, be reduced to "mere personality." Abigail offers a gift to David, perhaps the very protection money which Nabal refused (v. 27). She asks to be forgiven (v. 28).

Abigail then pronounces a sweeping dynastic promise. "The LORD will certainly make my lord a sure house" (25:28). How odd! In this story David is only the leader of a raiding band; Abigail, however, knows the future story,

knows David, knows in what larger story she is now in-
volved. Trusting in Yahweh's promise, Abigail does not
doubt that this bandit will become king. In desperate self-
interest, she suggests, it will be far more desirable for David
to arrive at the throne unclouded by complicity in the death
of Nabal. Because of the goodness and faithfulness of Yahweh to David, David's future need not be secured through
any violence perpetrated by David (v. 30). "My lord will
have no cause of grief, no pangs of conscience, for having
shed blood without cause or for my lord taking vengeance
himself" (v. 31). Abigail is sure that David will become king.
She is equally sure that it will be better for David to be a
king who is innocent of violence and vengeance. There is, in
fact, violence in this narrative. The rise of David is linked to
much violence but it is not David's. David's avoidance of
bloodguilt is a theological matter; it is also a practical political necessity. David could not begin his rule in a bloodbath,
for then governance would be impossible. The narrative
tells how circumstances conspired in David's favor.

The main focus of the narrative is on Yahweh's oversight
of vengeance. The narrative has a theological intention. As a
counterpoint, however, Abigail, the speaker of the dynastic
oracle, is also an important agent in the narrative. Almost as
a throwaway line, Abigail adds, "When the LORD has dealt
well with my lord, then remember your handmaid" (25:31).
In such an intensely Yahwistic account, Abigail is crucial. It
is she who enacts the restraint of Yahweh. It is she who
stands between David and bloodguilt. It is she who gives
voice to David's dynastic future. It is she who finally rescues
David from his propensity to violence. No wonder Abigail
has a claim on David's future, for she has made his future
possible.

David is convinced by the argument of Abigail and is
grateful for her rescue. His threat to murder, which he
vowed in 25:22, is now banished from his thought. His
thinking has been transformed by the intervention of Abigail. It is Abigail who has tamed his brutality. Her action is
credited as the action of Yahweh, who has in fact led David
away from his proposed brutality. David now senses an-

other, better way to proceed to power, a way proposed by Abigail, a way enacted by the Lord. Abigail functions in chapter 25 much as David's own noble resolve functions in chapters 24 and 26. She functions to break the direct, destructive confrontation between David and Nabal. The plot is broken by the assertion of God's governance, for Yahweh alone will work vengeance.[12]

David's response to Abigail (25:32–35) indicates his acceptance of Abigail's new reading of his situation. He begins in doxology:

> Blessed be the LORD, the God of Israel, who sent you this day to meet me! Blessed be your discretion, and blessed be you, who have kept me this day from bloodguilt, and from avenging myself with my own hand!

Verse 34 is a reiteration of what David had intended in verse 22. Thanks to Abigail, David now realizes that the action he had proposed to take against Nabal was ominous and future-forfeiting. David is astonished both at his own dangerous impetuousness and at Abigail's remarkable intervention, which can only be attributed to Yahweh. David dismisses Abigail with a benediction and an assurance (v. 35):

> Go up in peace. . . .
> I have hearkened to your voice, and
> I have granted your petition.

We are then told that Nabal died (25:37–38). His death is not a surprise. He had resisted David, which assured that his life was in jeopardy. Nabal's heart died; ten days later he died, having been killed by his own orgy of satiation. Yahweh smote Nabal (v. 38). David need not act to secure his own future. Yahweh is inscrutably at work dealing decisively with David's antagonists. Both David's vow to kill Nabal

---

[12]George M. Mendenhall, "The 'Vengeance' of Yahweh," in his *The Tenth Generation: The Origins of the Biblical Tradition* (Baltimore: Johns Hopkins University Press, 1973), 69–104, has shown that Yahweh's "vengeance" is in fact the orderly assertion of a comprehensive governance with sanctions sufficient to maintain sovereignty. Yahweh's "vengeance" is not capricious or arbitrary anger.

(v. 22) and his promise to Abigail to heed her (v. 35) have been fulfilled v. 39):

> Blessed be Yahweh who has avenged the insult . . . , and has kept back [ḥśk] his servant from evil; the LORD has returned the evil-doing of Nabal upon his own head.

Yahweh is at work to give David a better future than David can seize or initiate for himself.

Finally, David heeds Abigail's petition, "Remember your handmaid" (25:31). David remembers. He woos Abigail and takes her (vs. 39–40). The actions of the narrative have effected the transfer of Abigail to David and the elimination of Nabal. Underneath that plot, however, there has also been the odd, decisive intervention of Yahweh. Yahweh is thrust by the narrative between David and Nabal. As a result of Yahweh's decisive but hidden intervention, Nabal is destroyed and David is kept innocent. Nabal deserved to die because he resisted David, and he did die. But David did not murder.

These three narratives together (chs. 24–26) focus the David story on the troubling issue of the violence, murder, and vengeance that normally accompany a seizure or transfer of public power. In our reading of the narratives, we might have missed this accent, both because of the hidden working of Yahweh's vengeance, which guards David from bloodguilt, and because we have habitually read the text so benignly. These narratives show how close David lives to murderous action, tempted by his men (ch. 24), by Abishai (ch. 26), by his own rage (ch. 25). David is close to vengeance. He stops abruptly short, however, because he is confident of Yahweh's overriding purpose. These narratives assert the temptation of David and the innocence of David. He is as one "tempted in all things" but, in this narrative at least, "sinless" (cf. Heb. 4:15). I would not want to force any "Christological" connection here, nor do I suggest that the narrator has any such connection in mind. It occurs to me, nonetheless, that David is portrayed, albeit playfully, in a mode of acute innocence. When the New Testament comes to characterize Jesus in the same way, the claim is made absolute and all the narrative playfulness has disappeared. The contrast makes one wonder if the playful rendering of David was not a required precursor for the sobered, heightened claims of the New Testament.

Each of these three narratives is structured around two decisive affirmations. The same affirmations occur in all three narratives:

1. David is indeed destined for power. In each narrative this affirmation is placed in the mouth of David's main narrative partner:

> *Saul* in 24:20: "And now, behold, I know that you shall surely be king, and that the kingdom of Israel shall be established in your hand."
>
> *Abigail* in 25:28: "For the LORD will certainly make my lord a sure house, because my lord is fighting the battles of the LORD."
>
> *Saul* in 26:25: "Blessed be you, my son David! You will do many things and will succeed in them."

Even David's resisters must make this acknowledgment of David's future. In this way the narratives serve the larger story in presenting David's destiny as king.

2. It is the second affirmation that is unexpected, namely, David's innocence. David will arrive at royal power unencumbered by guilt:

> *Saul* in 24:17: "You are more righteous than I; for you have repaid me good, whereas I have repaid you evil."
>
> *Abigail* in 25:31: "My lord shall have no cause of grief, or pangs of conscience, for having shed blood without cause or for my lord taking vengeance himself."
>
> *David* in 26:23: "The LORD rewards every man for his righteousness and his faithfulness, for the LORD gave you into my hand today, and I would not put forth my hand against the LORD's anointed." [See Saul's parallel comment in v. 21.]

David is *ṣaddîq* (24:17; 26:23). David has been restrained from bloodguilt and from taking vengeance (25:26). David is innocent as he draws closer to power.

Bloodguilt Denied

In a second cluster of narratives, the issue of bloodguilt, violence, and innocence is more problematic for David. In 2 Samuel 1–4, David is now much closer to power. Saul is dead and Saul's political movement is in the last stages of collapse. In rapid succession, we learn of the death of Saul (ch. 1); of Abner, Saul's general (ch. 3); and of Ishbosheth, Saul's son and heir (ch. 4).[13] The presentation of the three deaths of Saul, Abner, and Ishbosheth have striking similarities and commonality of theme. The deaths accomplished in these narratives are convenient to David.[14] In each case David could readily be implicated or suspected of complicity. In each case, however, elaborate narrative provision is made to assert David's innocence and, conversely, to identify the true murderer, who must be brought to public account.

The Death of Saul: 2 Samuel 1.[15] This narrative sets the pattern for the deaths to come. A man (an Amalekite!) comes into David's camp (v. 2). He reports on the deaths of Saul and Jonathan (v. 4). When pressed, he claims he killed Saul (v. 10). He imagines he had done David a good turn in elimi-

---

[13]In the midst of the narrative concerning these three deaths, the murder of Asahel, the son of Zeruiah, is also reported (2 Sam. 2). That killing, however, is not pertinent to our study, for there is no thought that David is related to that killing or that David needs to be cleared of it.

[14]Abner's death did indeed eliminate a powerful hindrance to David, for Abner is now the main force of the Saulide movement. Abner, however, is presented not simply as a hindrance but also as a willing, valuable instrument for David. Thus, in the case of Abner, we cannot unambiguously state that his death was convenient to David, though his death clearly is not without that dimension for David.

[15]I am treating the death of Saul in 2 Sam. 1 as a literary counterpart to the other deaths in chapters 3 and 4. It is important to note that most scholars credit the first version of Saul's death in 1 Sam. 31 as being historically reliable, whereas the report in 2 Sam. 1 is not regarded as historically correct. However that may be, the literary presentation in chapter 1 is closely parallel to chapters 3 and 4. Moreover, in chapter 1 itself, no hint is given that the report of the Amalekite is regarded as a fabrication.

nating Saul and proudly brings to David Saul's crown and armlet, symbols of royal authority.

The man had badly miscalculated and misunderstood David, however. Upon learning of Saul's death, David immediately laments (1:11–12). David is savage in his interrogation of the man. "How is it you were not afraid to put forth your hand to destroy the LORD's anointed?" (v. 14). No chance is given for the man to answer. David does not linger but immediately orders his own men to kill the intruder: "Go, fall upon him" (v. 15). David's verdict is clear and unambiguous (v. 16):

> Your blood be upon your head; for your own mouth has testified against you, saying, "I have slain the LORD's anointed."

David's prompt and vigorous action assigns the bloodguilt for Saul's death unambiguously. In order to distance himself from any question of such guilt, David identifies himself with the death by an eloquent exhibition of grief. Thus grief, a perfectly credible response, is presented in the narrative as an innocent counterpart to guilt. David grieves an eloquent, public grief (1:19–27). The two acts of assigning bloodguilt to the Amalekite and grieving serve to clear David of any complicity in Saul's death.

The Death of Abner: 2 Samuel 3. We are told in passing in 3:1 that David is "stronger and stronger" and the Saul movement continues to fail. Of Saul's house and Saul's threat to David, nothing is left but the weak heir Ishbosheth and the towering Abner, who is the real power of the Saul movement. Abner is Ishbosheth's general. In verses 6–10, Abner challenges Ishbosheth, first by the dramatic act of seizing a royal concubine (vs. 7–8), and then, when rebuked, by a defiant, daring speech in which Abner vows the transfer of power and loyalty to David (vs. 9–10). Abner has embodied the main Saulide resistance to David, and he will now become the tool of Saulide capitulation to David. In turning to David, Abner asserts that he is only implementing what Yahweh has in fact already promised to David (v. 9). Abner claims only to be acting out Yahweh's resolve. It is convenient that Yahweh's resolve fits so comfortably Abner's own arrogant challenge to Ishbosheth. Abner is so powerful and so dangerous that Ishbosheth is forced to silence in the face of Abner's defiance (v. 11).

Abner negotiates with David (3:12–13a). Abner may be acting out Yahweh's intent, but to the Saulide party, Abner is unambiguously a traitor. David tests Abner's commitment to him by requiring return of his wife Michal, Saul's daughter, as a gesture of good faith. Abner passes the test; the wife is returned (vs. 13b–16). The delicate negotiations between Abner and David, between north and south, between the old regime and the new movement, are successful. David finds Abner enormously useful to his consolidation of power (vs. 17–19).

The narrator takes great pains to establish and reiterate exactly the condition of Abner as he left the court of David. Three times the narrator is careful to assert that Abner went from David in peace (*šalôm*). "He went in peace . . . He had gone in peace . . . It was told Joab, ' . . . He has gone in peace' " (3:21–23). The care and detail of these verses show that the narrator wants to be precise about Abner's condition. The narrator wants to establish a reliable witness on David's behalf to show that Abner was uninjured and unimpeded as he left David. Whatever damage was done to Abner was done *after* he was with David. Afterward, when the killing happened, David is absent; Joab is very much present and implicated. This distinction of Abner with David and Abner with Joab is established not only by the later words of David (vs. 28–29) but by the "objective" report of the narrator. Thus the "peace" of Abner is linked to the innocence of David.

Joab is David's Ed Meese. Upon hearing of the negotiations between David and Abner, Joab is enraged. He no doubt perceives Abner as a threat to his own preeminence with David. He also perceives Abner as a threat to David, for he does not trust Abner's intention or motive (3:24–25). Joab, always looking after what he perceives as David's best interests, is quick and decisive. He kills Abner (v. 27). In doing so, he jeopardizes the entire northern project of David. Our interest, however, is in the twofold response of David to the killing.

First, David publicly establishes guilt for the murder (3:28–29):

> I and my kingdom are for ever guiltless before the LORD for the death of Abner the son of Ner. May it fall upon the head of Joab, and upon all his father's house; and may the house of Joab never be without one who has a discharge, or who is leprous, or who holds a spindle, or who is slain by the sword, or who lacks bread!

This is an incredibly poignant and comprehensive curse. The depth of the curse is no doubt commensurate with the significance of Abner, his political power in the north, and Abner's potential usefulness to David. Abner's death has struck very close to David's throne. David passionately distances himself from the vengefulness of his own chief of staff.

Second, David's curse is matched by a public show of grief (3:31–39). David lowers the flags, leads the mourning, gives a state funeral. Above all, he requires Joab to join the public funeral, for "a great man has fallen this day in Israel" (vs. 31, 38). At the end of the chapter, David in a soliloquy says, "The LORD requite (*šlm*) the evildoer according to his wickedness!" (v. 39). David's self-serving speech is aimed at Joab, who is "the evildoer." Such confident piety on David's part is good politics, for he can distance himself from Joab's self-serving killing. By the statement, Joab should be executed promptly. He is not, perhaps for practical reasons: Joab is too important and too powerful. David and the narrator, however, have a long, durable memory (cf. 1 Kings 1:5–7; 2:28–34). Just retribution may take a long time. But it is sure, and the narrative can be very patient. Again, political motives notwithstanding, the narrator uses the words of David to situate the death of Abner in the framework of moral retribution. David is scrupulous in acknowledging the moral coherence of the world in which these deaths happen. There must be payment for Abner's death; it will not be David, however, who will pay.

The Death of Ishbosheth: 2 Samuel 4. The death of
Ishbosheth is almost predictable and anticlimactic. It is as
though we are waiting for the narrator to tell us how Saul's
party finally loses everything. Without Abner, Ishbosheth is
politically and militarily irrelevant. David, however, has
made a sure oath to Jonathan to honor the offspring of Saul's
house, so David cannot destroy this last obstacle to power
(1 Sam. 20:12–17).

Despite David's oath, however, Ishbosheth is killed. Two
of David's young turks enact yet another death convenient
for David (4:5–7). The death of Ishbosheth is violent: "They
smote him . . . they slew him . . . they beheaded him." The
two bring the head of Ishbosheth as a trophy to David
(vs. 7–8). Like the Amalekite in chapter 1, they imagine
they are doing David a favor and anticipate a commendation,
if not a reward. They present the head to David with self-
congratulation: "The LORD has avenged my lord the king
this day on Saul and on his offspring" (v. 8). They interpret
their own work as the vengeance of Yahweh.

This death is in fact the last thing David needs just now.
Without Abner, David is already winning against the Saulide
party. He does not need to alienate the remnants of Saul
sentiment. David looks past the immediate death to his political future and responds to their cynical presentation
(4:9–11):

> As Yahweh lives, who has redeemed my life from every adver-
> sity, when one told me, "Behold, Saul is dead," and thought he
> was bringing good news, I seized him and slew him at Ziklag,
> which was the reward I gave him for his news. How much
> more, when wicked men have slain a righteous man in his own
> house upon his bed, shall I not now require his blood at your
> hand, and destroy you from the earth?

David has the killers publicly hanged to exhibit their guilt
(v. 12). The counterpart of David's innocence in this narrative is not elaborate, but it is present. David gives an honor-
able burial to Ishbosheth's head in his own city of Hebron
(v. 12).

In the process of telling of these three deaths, the narrator permits David to emerge as politically stronger than he was, and theologically vindicated. At least in these narratives, David has managed these three deaths without any personal involvement. The repeated need to assert innocence and to identify the culprit in such public and punitive terms indicates that the deaths are a potential danger to David and to his future. In each case, bloodguilt is explicitly assigned:

Your blood be upon your head. (1:16)

I and my kingdom are forever guiltless before the Lord of the blood of Abner, son of Ner. May it fall on the head of Joab. (3:28–29)

"Shall I not now require his blood at your hand?" (4:11)

The throne rests on blood and violence. That violence, however, is not the doing of David. The killing each time is done by someone else, who imagines either that he is loyal to David or is acting out the intent of Yahweh. The narrative pays enormous attention to the issue of bloodguilt.

Once More, Acquittal

These two cycles of 1 Samuel 24–26 and 2 Samuel 1–4 are clearly arranged in thematic groupings. Both cycles advance David's cause. Both, as I have shown, are troubled about David's temptation to violence, killing, vengeance, and guilt. In 1 Samuel 24–26, the violence and vengeance are resisted, as David violates neither Saul nor Nabal. In 2 Samuel 1–4, there is ample blood-shedding and therefore guilt, but the guilt cannot be assigned to David. In bloodguilt resisted and then denied, David escapes by a whisker from mortal danger. David's escape from guilt is clearly the intent of the narrative.

There are hints, however, that the narrative was not enough to persuade public opinion among David's contemporaries. In 2 Samuel 16:8, there is a note suggesting that David's careful, self-serving propaganda was not completely successful. Shimei, with old and deep loyalty to the Saulide cause, gives voice to a passionate anti-David opinion. He shouts at David (16:7–8):

> Begone, begone, you man of blood, you worthless fellow! The LORD has avenged upon you all the blood of the house of Saul, in whose place you have reigned; and the LORD has given the kingdom into the hand of your son Absalom. See, your ruin is on you; for you are a man of blood.

David has now arrived at power. The narrator wants to assert that David arrived at power because of God's firm resolve on David's behalf.

The narrator, however, cannot completely silence the public response of the losers who view David's grasp of power very differently.[16] David, and David's house, would like to silence the losers (cf. 2 Sam. 16:9). The narrator, however, will not permit such a silencing. There is a theological realism in the narrative. When brutality is committed, even by beloved David, it lingers and cries out for recompense. Losers characteristically do not blame their suffering on hidden providence, but on nameable historical agents who commit violence. Even David cannot obliterate the unanswered claims of his victims. Shimei voices a live Israelite opinion that David has arrived at power, not by spirit but by flesh and blood, not by the name of Yahweh but by sword and spear and javelin (contrast 1 Sam. 17:45). David's throne, it is asserted by Shimei, is not a gift of God's providence but a work of raw, brutal power. Shimei's voice is important because it attests that the pro-David "official" narrative did not completely persuade Israel. David needs a still more compelling acquittal.

The David narratives we have considered are at pains to maintain David's innocence of the blood that has been shed in Israel. Nonetheless, there must have been a continuing

---

[16]David M. Gunn, "David and the Gift of the Kingdom, 2 Sam. 2–4, 9–20, 1 Kgs. 1–2," *Semeia* 3 (1975): 14–45, has nicely articulated the dialectic of "gift" and "grasp" in the David narrative. On the whole, as Gunn argues, David is a creature of gift. The element of grasping, however, is not completely absent from the narrative.

residue of suspicion in ancient Israel concerning David and his establishment of power. The narrative of 1 Samuel 27–30, I submit, is shaped to meet the continuing need of David for acquittal. This narrative cycle concerns David's sojourn with the Philistines.

As a fugitive from Saul, David plays a dangerous game of alliance with the Philistines, Israel's great and perennial enemy. David is a gambler playing for high stakes, for the entire episode runs the risk of treasonable cooperation with the enemy. The fact that David enters such an alliance at all indicates how much at risk his life and movement are, and how few options he has available to him in the face of Saul's pursuit.

The tension in this narrative turns on three points in 1 Samuel 27.

1. David makes raids on the Geshurites, Girzites, and Amalekites, Israel's traditional enemies (27:8). There is nothing objectionable for Israel in this. David is ruthless in these raids, takes no prisoners, leaves no witnesses.

2. David lies to his trusting Philistine host, Achish (27:10). David does not tell Achish that he is conducting raids against Israel's enemies. Rather he lies and tells his host that he is raiding Judah, the Jerahmeelites, and the Kenites, peoples allied with the Israelite movement. The discrepancy between the actual object of the raids (v. 8) and the reported object of the raids (v. 10) is important for the narrative that is to follow.

3. This deception is the hinge of the narrative. David raids in ways compatible with Judean loyalties. David has an eye on his Israelite constituency, and he will not risk that constituency in order to please the Philistines. David represents himself to Achish, however, as acting against his own people. On the basis of this disinformation, Achish concludes David is trustworthy for the Philistines, because, having become abhorrent to Israel, David has no alternative place to go (27:12). The narrative proceeds from this massive, deliberate, and effective falsehood.

The danger to David in his double-agent game is escalated in 1 Samuel 28:1-2 when the Philistines are about to go to

war with the Israelites. As long as there was no direct conflict between the two peoples, David could sneak by without
a public risk or a public decision. Now, however, there will
be war between Israel and the Philistines; David must de-
cide. Either he must fight with the Philistines and be seen as
an enemy to his own people, or he must refuse to fight
against his own people and lose his place among the Philistines.

The risk for David becomes even greater when Achish
elevates David to be his personal bodyguard, making David
enormously visible (28:1–2). As head of the bodyguard, David is especially trusted by Achish, but he is also under acute
surveillance. In verse 2 David agrees to this special role.

The narrative delays. We are made to wait while Saul has
his last, desperate rendezvous with the dead Samuel (28:3–
25). That episode is resolved in the clear verdict of the dead
Samuel: "The LORD has torn the kingdom out of your hand,
and given it to your neighbor, David" (v. 17).[17] The narrative now grows exceedingly taut as the demise of Saul and
the make-or-break situation of David are set in juxtaposition. Perhaps the throne will finally be given to David, as
Samuel has decreed. At the same time, however, David appears to have exhausted his uncommon luck.[18] David, with
the Philistines, is in a place from which there seems to be no
extrication. The tension between Samuel's decree and David's circumstance is acute. At best we may expect, on the
basis of Samuel's powerful affirmation, that Yahweh will intervene to save David.

When David and Achish resume their conversation in

---

[17]1 Sam. 28:17 is surely an intentional reference back to 1 Sam. 13:14. In
the earlier passage, David is not explicitly named but only an allusion to
him is offered. By the later passage, the narrative has advanced enough so
that the designation of David can, both for political and artistic reasons,
now be made explicit.

[18]Lore Segal, "II Samuel," in *Congregation: Contemporary Writers Read
the Jewish Bible*, ed. David Rosenberg (New York: Harcourt Brace Jova-
novich, 1987), 108 writes: "The subtle story makes him something of both:
David is a righteous man who has God's grace, meaning the world's good
luck, and his luck is running out—it will run out in its time."

1 Samuel 29, a new voice enters the narrative, one not previously known or expected. It is the voice of the Philistine
overlords, the really big boys in the Philistine power structure (29:2–3). It turns out that Achish is a subservient agent
for the overlords. The top generals are cunning and discern-
ing. Unlike Achish, the top generals are not so easily taken
in by David. They are much more suspicious about David,
because they have received intelligence reports about the
"thousands and ten thousands" (vs. 4–5). They conclude
that because David is popular in Israel, he is a high risk for
the Philistines. Thus, David may not fight for the Philistines
against Israel, and he might double-cross.

We had imagined David would be rescued from his dilemma by Yahweh. Yahweh, however, is completely absent
in this narrative. Practical political events are permitted to
work themselves out. Taken by itself, this episode is simply
human drama. Taken in context, God is absent only on the
surface of the narrative. The narrative has prepared us for
the judgment that whenever David's future is at stake, the
power of Yahweh is not far away. Thus we expect that Yahweh's absence in this episode is a mode of deeply hidden
presence. The narrative is pure politics. David is rescued
only by the wise suspicion of the Philistine generals who
overrule Achish. David is saved, not because he is God's
messiah, but because he is a potential turncoat. David is delivered from his dilemma by a Philistine refusal to let him
fight; but then, Yahweh's providence is always hidden.

Achish is the man in the middle. He is personally loyal to
David, believes in David's trustworthiness, and accepts David's deception as true. Achish, however, is unable to act on
his conviction or loyalty to David. Achish is overridden by
the leadership and he must accept their decision.

Achish has now been firmly overruled by his overlords.
Nonetheless he still has an important function in this narrative. Three times he asserts David's innocence:

1. In 29:3, Achish testifies to the overlords, "I have found
no fault in him to this day."
2. In 29:6, Achish says the same thing to David: "I have

found nothing wrong in you from the day of your coming to me to this day."

3. In 29:9, when David presses Achish for the data concerning his dismissal, Achish is led to say a third time, "I know that you are as blameless in my sight as an angel of God; nevertheless . . . "

David is not permitted to fight with the Philistines. David is sent safely back to Ziklag, away from the battle (1 Sam. 29:11–30:1). David is delivered from the critical moment when he is at risk. David is saved from the terrible options he faced, saved by unwitting Philistine intervention. Until that intervention, David either had to side with the Philistines against his own people or be eliminated by the Philistines as an enemy. Now, however, the crisis has passed. He need not choose.

I submit that by this odd, unexpected turn, David received the additional rhetorical acquittal required by the avoided bloodguilt of 2 Samuel 24–26 and the denied bloodguilt of 2 Samuel 1–4. Thus Achish's threefold formula of acquittal in 1 Samuel 29 has a larger aim in the narrative than simply the Philistine episode. The formula of acquittal hovers over the entire narrative to affirm about David concerning Saul and Nabal (1 Sam. 24–26), concerning Saul, Abner, and Ishbosheth (2 Sam. 1–4): "There is no guilt in the man." The verdict is a rhetorical response to the old Saulide suspicion voiced by Shimei. David is an innocent man. No one has found evidence against him. He is exonerated on the lips of an unwitting, trusting, gullible Philistine.

But what kind of acquittal is it? It is not a judicial acquittal. It is a narrative acquittal, which means it is not straightforward, not precise, but playful, teasing, seductive, inviting the kind of winking ambiguity that always attends David.[19]

---

[19]Thus chapter 29 presents the question of David's guilt and innocence with high irony, so that what is said is in tension with what is intended. On the ironic dimension of biblical narrative, see Gail R. O'Day, *Revelation in the Fourth Gospel: Narrative Mode and Theological Claim* (Philadelphia: Fortress Press, 1986).

The acquittal operates in Israel's narrative imagination in a suggestive but ambivalent way.

On the face of it, David is acquitted. Achish means what he says three times. Given the public facts with which Achish works, the acquittal is authentic. We, however, know more than Achish knows. We know David is a double-dealer and so in fact is guilty. Thus David is ostensibly innocent, but manifestly guilty. We can, however, press behind this ambiguity one step further. The story is not for Philistine hearing. In fact, whether David is innocent or guilty by Philistine norms is irrelevant to the narrative and to the ears of intended Israelite listeners. In those Israelite ears, it did not matter at all if David had lied to the Philistines and had been treacherous. Indeed, it is all the better for David if in fact he had deceived the enemy. Israel could take comfort and delight from the awareness that David has duped the Philistines. The very duplicity which made David guilty to the Philistines in fact commends him to Israel and makes him boldly, compellingly innocent, measured not by petty morality, but by the nerve and chutzpah to confound the arrogant enemy.[20] David's innocence in the narrative is not according to an absolute norm, but according to the well-being and future of Israel and God's rule, which requires outwitting and outflanking the despised, uncircumcised Philistines.

Thus, in the end Achish, deceived and without correct data, does have it right about David. For reasons Achish could never understand (because he has no access to Israel's faith), he is correct in saying that there is no guilt in David. David has kept faith with Israel on the large issues. David is

[20]The David-Goliath narrative thus serves as a paradigm for David's mastery of "the Philistine problem." The narrative of 1 Sam. 17 is well placed at the very outset of the David story. Whether David is historically linked to Goliath or not (see 2 Sam. 21:19) is irrelevant, for the tradition-building process has articulated the enduring public claim of David in Israel around this triumph. Whatever else Israel knows about David, it knows David is capable of handling the Philistines, not only by power and courage, but also by cunning and deception.

an utterly faithful man, as righteous as Saul announces (1 Sam. 24:17), as free of pangs of conscience as Abigail anticipates (25:31), as uncontaminated by bloodguilt as David himself repeatedly asserts (cf. 26:18). Achish has given a true and faithful verdict, even though it is for all the wrong reasons.[21]

Narrative Portrayal and Proclaimed Alternative

At this point, I would like to press beyond textual exposition to suggest a connection to the practice of ministry. On the basis of this exploration, I want to offer some reflections on narrative as a way of acknowledging and transforming the violence and brutality that moves just below the surface of our life. Interpretation and proclamation of these texts consists in the retelling of the narrative. But to what end?

The purpose of such narratives retold is not to review a history lesson about David, certainly not to champion the heroism of David as a moral figure, nor to celebrate the ar-

---

[21]This threefold verdict of acquittal seems to me to reverberate in the Lukan and Johannine accounts of Jesus' trial before Pilate. Pilate is also a man in the middle, caught between his own conviction of the innocence of Jesus, and the overpowering interest and threat of Rome. Pilate also three times gives the verdict, "I find no guilt in him" (Luke 23:4, 14–15, 22; John 18:38; 19:4, 6). Pilate, like Achish, gives the right verdict for the wrong reason. In fact, Pilate completely misunderstands, as does Achish, for Jesus is indeed the sworn enemy and subverter of all in which Pilate trusts. As 1 Sam. 29 is not set down for Achish's benefit, so the narrative of Jesus' trial is not told for Pilate's consumption. It is a tale for the followers of Jesus, who observe that in Jesus' subversive undermining of worldly authority, Jesus is surely to be judged a traitor. In the end, however, Jesus is in fact innocent and in the service of the purposes of God. Pilate, like Achish, understands much less than he imagines but unwittingly gives the right verdict. Pilate gives a verdict on the basis of evidence the world can evaluate. He gives a verdict the world can neither understand nor accept. In this second case, as well, the accused man is three times declared innocent, and then treated as guilty. See my analysis of the parallels between the David narrative and the trial of Jesus in "Narrative Intentionality in I Samuel 29," *JSOT* 43 (1989): 21–35. Wayne C. Booth, *A Rhetoric of Irony* (Chicago: University of Chicago Press, 1974), 28–29, 91–93, has suggested ironic elements in the rendering of Jesus' trial.

rival of God's kingdom through David. There is in these texts a matter much more immediate to us, if we have wits and imagination. The narratives illuminate the disease, ambiguity, and prospect of our own life. When the narrative is retold, it could happen that our own lives are also decisively retold with candor, perceptiveness, and possibility. Moreover, when retold imaginatively, our lives in the process may be redescribed, resignified, and transformed.

Such retelling might aid us in getting the central questions of our life focused. In the managerial and therapeutic models of life critically explicated by Robert Bellah and company,[22] we tend to screen out *the savage, ominous power of violence and vengeance,* the will to retaliate, the drive to hurt and to get even, and the sad inescapable truth that much of our well-being is conditioned by an invisible but brutal darkness. The narrative does not flinch from the constant, besetting temptation to violence and the seductions surrounding that temptation.

Mostly, our bourgeois discernments of human life are governed by Enlightenment perceptions in which morality is chooseable, life is a set of problems to be solved, and manageable possibilities are all that are in purview. Against that self-deception so powerful in our culture, the voice of the biblical text is one of the few compelling witnesses to the "tradition of darkness" which Freud, Marx, and Nietzsche exposed,[23] that tradition which is deeper, older, and more powerful than they themselves reckoned.

---

[22]Robert N. Bellah et al., *Habits of the Heart: Individualism and Commitment in American Life* (Berkeley: University of California Press, 1985), has provided a splendid analysis of the pathology of therapeutic and managerial consciousness in our society. In focusing on these two themes, Bellah follows Alasdair MacIntyre, *After Virtue: A Study in Moral Theory,* 2nd ed. (Notre Dame: University of Notre Dame Press, 1984).

[23]In *Freud and Philosophy: An Essay on Interpretation* (New Haven: Yale University Press, 1970), Paul Ricoeur has focused on "suspicion" as an interpretive practice. In his *The Symbolism of Evil* (Boston: Beacon Press, 1969), Ricoeur has recognized that the darkness is not merely an interpretive problem but is constitutive of the human situation. See Douglas J. Hall, *Lighten Our Darkness: Toward an Indigenous Theology of the Cross* (Phila-

The power of that darkness is not a fresh insight of modern thought. The Bible has long known about the seething brutality mostly right beneath the surface of public life. That dread darkness which seduces us into brutality relates to public policy questions of arms and nuclear possibility, to public outcries for capital punishment, and to rage that comes dressed as reason. The thirst to kill in order to control also takes place in the intimacy of marriage, in the conflict of siblings, in the bureaucracy of the church. That untamed, eager brutishness finally is part of who we are. The narrative of David holds our attention because it has as its subject our own life, a life not resolved and simple, but a life raw, unresolved, ruthless. We are always close to blood, either as perpetrator or as victim, in both cases overwhelmed by a violence we can neither justify or deny and which we mostly leave unacknowledged.

The narrative keeps posing the question about *moral possibility* in the midst of all our seduction to violence and vengeance. Abigail speaks of restraint and "pangs of conscience." David and Saul converse about "righteousness and faithfulness." David, Saul, and Abigail, to say nothing of Joab, however, are not romantic about these matters. They do not imagine for an instant that faithfulness and righteousness are easy, obvious, chooseable choices. These are choices always surrounded by fear, greed, hate, and revenge, choices taken in great danger and at great risk, requiring not only nobility but trusting, submitting, and yielding. These narratives bespeak a wistful longing for another life that could be lived with a singleness of vision that is driven by neither rage nor fear. David holds our imagination because he acts out this vision of another life, not overcome by his thirst for dominance.

These narratives invite us to notice and name *the Absent One* who is so powerfully present in the course of the story.[24] It may be only stylized speech always to invoke the

delphia: Westminster Press, 1976). In Luther, with "the perversion of reason," the interpretive and constitutive darknesses are of a piece.

[24]On the present/absent one, see Samuel L. Terrien, *The Elusive Pres-*

name of Yahweh as does the narrative. The frequent reference to Yahweh, however, permits the imagination to discern that there is another party at work in the midst of the seething of brutality. At bottom, David and Abigail believe there is another one who declares, "Vengeance is mine" (cf. 1 Sam. 25:39). This is not to pretend that David's personal world is an innocent world where human vengeance is not necessary or operative. There is indeed vengeance in David's world, as Nabal learned, but it is a vengeance left at last to the powerful faithfulness of Yahweh. That conviction affirmed by the narrative permits a vigorous articulation of the moral seriousness of Yahweh. It is, however, a moral seriousness finally determined by God, and not preempted by us.

It is God, and not David, who finally must requite Saul, Nabal, the Amalekite, Joab, Baanah, and Rechab. David neither can nor must resolve their destructiveness. Yahweh is at work, adjudicating righteousness and wickedness. Yahweh's work may be hidden or indirect, as in the intervention of unwitting Philistine overlords. Or Yahweh's work may be through a human agent like Abigail. In the end, nevertheless, it is Yahweh's governance which is decisive.

In the end, *the matters of justification, innocence, acquittal, and vindication* are at the center of the story. The narrative drips with danger. Shimei may have it right. In the end, David might have to ask, "If you, O LORD, shouldst mark iniquities, LORD, who could stand?" (Ps. 130:3). Well, none could stand, certainly not David. Yet perhaps David and all those who travel with David could "stand," because God has sworn fidelity and works well-being for David. Perhaps David finally turns out to be "righteous" because he is willing to leave vengeance in the hands of Yahweh and will not usurp what is not rightly his.

By the curious route of narrative realism, we are back to the old, grand theme of righteousness and justification. We did not, however, arrive there by legalism and moralism and

ence: Toward a New Biblical Theology (San Francisco: Harper & Row, 1978).

"tortured conscience," or by "sinners in the hands of an angry God."[25] The theme of justification is not a purely religious theme of guilt, guilty conscience, and alienation from God, as it has been explicated in the Augustinian-Lutheran tradition.

Characteristically for the Old Testament, the issue of righteousness before God is much more linked to the public world, much more concerned with neighbor and political reality, with power and brutality, violence, and vengeance, and the counter themes of trust, submission, and waiting. As this narrative asserts, David is finally a righteous man. His righteousness, however, is not rooted in David's action, but in the overriding Presence that seems always to guard David and intervene on his behalf. In a subtle, understated way, the narrative of Samuel is not about David, but about the One whose larger purposes can be and are served in the midst of much self-serving. For all his political realism, David finds ways of yielding to purposes that called him beyond himself.

We ponder this David narrative, because our lives are like the life of David. We are always on the way to power, brooding in the darkness, sometimes turning from the darkness to the astonishing gift of life. Matters in our lives are endlessly distorted by these sorry, tempting realities. We are hopeless and helpless to extricate ourselves from the greedy anxiety that drives us. Our problem is not that we want to kill God, whom we have not seen. It is rather that we want to kill our brother and sister whom we have seen (1 John 4:20).

We attend to this dreadful theme in this powerful narrative, because there is so much here which we are prone to deny. The acknowledgment of, embrace of, and transformation of that dark, powerful reality is nearly lost in our romantic, emotive culture. Until the ominous reality of

[25]On the characteristic "Lutheran" inclination toward a "tortured conscience," see Krister Stendahl, "The Apostle Paul and the Introspective Conscience of the West," *Harvard Theological Review* 56 (1963): 199–215, reprinted in his *Paul Among the Jews and Gentiles, and Other Essays* (Philadelphia: Fortress Press, 1976), 78–96.

violence is faced, however, the Gospel is not much more than a bit of "self-help" that conspires in our romantic self-deception. The narrative leads us to a reality about ourselves that we may want to deny. It does not stop there, however; it also leads us through that reality, accompanied by the God who moves in the reality and works new purpose there. The narrative tells us of another righteousness wrought on our behalf. It does more than tell us of it. It also mediates that new righteousness as we join in the narrative.

The vindication of David given in the narrative is ambiguous. The verdict of Achish in 1 Samuel 29 is an example of our situation in which *the ambiguity is so transparent.* The right verdict is given by Achish, but it is given for all the wrong reasons. Even after Achish's threefold acquittal, there is still terrible ambivalence, for it is an acquittal based on false data for the wrong reasons. We are left with a powerful uneasiness about David and the strange, hidden alliance between Yahweh and the Philistine overlords that oddly works good for David (cf. Rom. 8:28).

Our life is like that. The verdicts to which we have access are regularly ambiguous, often given for the wrong reasons. In that ambiguity, however, Yahweh's resilient fidelity is made visible by the narrator. It is that resilient fidelity which is the center of David's narrative. That same fidelity is the central theme of the narrative of our life, a fidelity wrought through elusive ambiguity.

My point is this: The narrative retold could help us recover the theme and nerve of evangelical preaching. Much of our preaching is like Churchill's pudding, i.e., it has no theme. We are reduced to liberal "good causes," or pious romanticism, or conservative moralism, all of which cover over the violence, hurt, hate, and ambiguity where we live. I would not make easy connections between text and the crisis of contemporary life. I do not believe the Bible functions so directly. (See my introductory comments on the interface of scripture and church). I do suggest, however, that the church's loss of its nerve and its theme for preaching is a massive, perhaps decisive, contribution to the brutality for which we have no adequate language. The abandonment of narrative imagination in the life of the church leaves us with sterile moral and theological options that end us in despair and exhaustion.

These David narratives suggest a quite different range of themes for interpretation and proclamation:

1. The *power of violence and vengeance* is among us.
2. The *moral possibility* can be wrought only at great risk.
3. The *absent One is powerfully present* in such comings and goings.
4. *Justification and well-being* that override our immobilizing destructiveness are topics that cannot be avoided.
5. The teasing ambiguity of *right verdicts for wrong reasons* is not remote from our experience, but it is an ambiguity in the service of a sovereign fidelity.

These same themes for interpretation and proclamation will make crucial contact with our more immediate local issues, our ignoble loyalties, our alienated covenants, our noble, shattered intentions, our grasping for power, our endless attempts to vindicate ourselves. These narratives offer no closed, simple resolutions of the human riddle. They invite, rather, a faithful living through. That living through is possible, however, only when the pathos of personhood, the rawness of power, and the hidden resilience of providence converge. Without all three, our lives are thinly deceptive. These stories guard our faith, our life, and our proclamation from being thin, comfortable, deceptive, and simplistic.

These stories bear witness to the Absent/Present One who

> will not always chide,
>   nor will he keep his anger forever. . . .
> As parents pity their children,
>   so the LORD pities those who fear God.
> For God knows our frame,
>   and remembers that we are dust.
> As for humankind, our days are like grass,
>   we flourish like a flower of the field;
>   for the wind passes over it, and it is gone,
>   and its place knows it no more.

> But the steadfast love of the LORD
>   is from everlasting to everlasting
>   upon those who fear God.
>   Psalm 103:9, 13–17; RSV alt.

The recital of this psalm about God's generous fidelity is a powerful voice in the faith of Israel. This psalm we love so much must be set, however, in the midst of the dangerous ambiguity of the narrative. The psalm makes faith clean and resolved; it gives an uncomplicated picture of Yahweh. The narrative, however, tells us otherwise. The God who does not keep anger forever permits a destructive range of anger in our life. The God who remembers that we are dust seems often unmindful and indifferent. The God of steadfast love seems often so long in coming that the world seems driven by fickleness.

David finally is the one who embodies the antiphon of Israel's faith, moving between the raw narrative and the sure psalm. The psalm by itself settles things too serenely. The narrative by itself drastically unsettles. It is, however, only in the full face of the unsettled, unsettling narrative that Israel's lyric of trust makes transformation sense. The church much prefers the psalm to the narrative. It is my urging that we must reenter the narrative, for only there can we touch the wildness, only there can we sound and hear and trust the song made especially for the night. The song of trust does not keep the narrative of night from being about the night. In the presence of the song of trust, however, the night becomes a transformed night. David had to learn that transformative truth, episode by episode. So can we. Our relearning, however, requires many retellings.

4

Pretensions to Royal Absolutism: An Alternative

At the end of the narrative of David in 2 Samuel, the king is now ensconced in Jerusalem, powerful, with a standing army, an extensive bureaucracy, an ample harem, an entrenched priesthood, an intricate tax system. The story had begun in the hopeful Song of Hannah about the power of Yahweh who "lifts the needy from the ash heap, to make them sit with princes" (1 Sam. 2:8).[1] In David, Yahweh has enacted that very inversion about which Hannah sang. David is an exhibit of Israel's conviction that Yahweh can bring low and raise up.

Emerging Royal Absolutism as a Narrative Achievement

In this discussion I will reflect on the state absolutism that emerged in Israel in the time of David and Solomon. That royal absolutism no doubt had an economic-political base. It commanded respect and obedience, however, because the emerging economic-political monopoly was given religious legitimation. While the political and economic factors are crucial in its emergence, here I will be concerned with the

---

[1]Brevard S. Childs, *Introduction to the Old Testament as Scripture* (Philadelphia: Fortress Press, 1979), 271–280, has shown us how to think of the wholeness of the story of Samuel and has suggested the ways in which the Song of Hannah gives us the themes of the story to follow.

problem of religious legitimacy.[2] Specifically, I will consider texts that seem concerned to delegitimate the regime, that is to withdraw the theological sanction without which it could not survive.

Along the way of David's astonishing transformation from shepherd boy (1 Sam. 16:11) to shepherd king (2 Sam. 5:2), something happened in Israel that was perhaps predictable.[3] The royal establishment appropriated political theory and political rationality that was common to the great empires of the Near East.[4] The Jerusalem establishment, under David or under Solomon, became comfortable with royal ideology and its accompanying power, prestige, and wealth. That ideology, however, was deeply alien to Israel's old covenantal tradition articulated by Moses and embodied in Samuel. Whereas that old covenant tradition at best accommodated royal power as a useful instrument of covenantalism (cf. Deut. 17:14–20), the royal ideology now made a very differ-

---

[2]On the political and economic factors related to the emergence of the Davidic monarchy, see Frank S. Frick, *The Formation of the State in Ancient Israel* (Sheffield: Almond Press, 1985). See now the full and comprehensive treatment of the data by James W. Flanagan, *David's Social Drama: A Hologram of Israel's Early Iron Age*, Social World of Biblical Antiquity, 7 (Sheffield: Almond Press, 1988).

[3]It is probable that the more decisive and ominous changes occurred in the reign of Solomon rather than in the time of David. David, however, is taken as a literary device for a portrayal of the Solomonic period. See Frank Moore Cross, *Canaanite Myth and Hebrew Epic* (Cambridge, Mass.: Harvard University Press, 1973), 229–241. Flanagan, *David's Social Drama*, makes the convincing case that David remains a tribal chieftain and intentionally resists the development of kingship. The emergence of the state with its higher view of kingship happened under Solomon, not under David. David shrewdly discerned what was politically possible and conducted himself accordingly.

[4]The extent to which Davidic-Solomonic Israel appropriated and embraced imperial ideology is a matter of continuing dispute. The most extreme case for appropriation has been made by Ivan Engnell, *Studies in Divine Kingship in the Ancient Near East* (Uppsala: Almqvist & Wiksell, 1943). See also Henri Frankfort, *Kingship and the Gods* (Chicago: University of Chicago Press, 1948); Aubrey R. Johnson, *Sacral Kingship in Ancient Israel* (Cardiff: University of Wales Press, 1956); and Cross, *Canaanite Myth and Hebrew Epic*, 241–273.

ent claim. Now kingship no longer belonged to the well-being *(bene esse)* of Israel, but to its being *(esse)*. Now kingship had become integral, essential, definitional, and indispensable for the life and character of Israel. The king became an embodiment of the life of Israel and rivaled or even displaced torah (the law) as the distinguishing, organizing principle of the community. The struggle between torah and kingship that marks Israel's monarchial period is a conflict between the old covenantalism and the new ideology that justified the royal monopoly of power.[5]

The narratives of David faithfully and carefully trace the emergence of David as king, seeing in his rise the work of the faithful promise and power of Yahweh. When the narrators complete the story, they are astonished, I think embarrassed, and perhaps even aghast at what has happened during the course of their narrative. The story ends with a king beset by self-serving political arrogance and autonomy. The transition from 2 Samuel to 1 Kings is unexpected. The end of the David story in 1 Kings 1–2 opens with a cynical dispute over the royal succession, with incredibly crass advice to Solomon from David about how to secure the throne by eliminating enemies and settling old debts, with a coup and a modest bloodbath. In the end, Solomon is "arrayed in all his glory," in all his arrogance, power, pride, and affluence. Clearly the foundations of Israel's life and worldview have changed.

The Old Testament is not of one mind about this transformation of public power in Israel. There is, to be sure, an appreciation of this new power and wealth as a gift from God. There is, however, at the same time an uneasiness with such power, for it comes to embody absolutism.

---

[5]The conflict in the monarchic period between the old covenantalism and the new ideology is especially articulated in the great confrontations between kings and prophets. It is, however, more subtly and programmatically presented in the Deuteronomists. In Deuteronomy, the prophets appeal to torah precisely to resist royal theology. In the end, however, Deuteronomy must make space for the legitimacy of royal theology, albeit guardedly.

A Covenantal Alternative to Royal Pretension

The material to which I refer as a text seeking to delegitimate royal absolutism is 2 Samuel 21–24. These chapters are commonly regarded as a miscellaneous collection of materials in an appendix, materials that have fallen out of chronological sequence. Very little scholarly work has been done on this material. Following Karl Budde,[6] it is conventional to observe that there are six elements arranged in chiastic fashion: two narratives, two lists, and two poems. That observation is correct but does not take us very far. We have still to ask, what is their literary function and intention in this particular place?

I propose that these four chapters stand as a counterpart to the materials in 2 Samuel 5–8. Chapters 5–8 and 21–24 both fall outside the two great narratives, the Rise of David and the Successive Narrative, posited by scholarship.[7] In a remarkable article, James Flanagan has proposed that 2 Samuel 5–8 consists in six elements chiastically arranged, two lists, two battle narratives, and two narratives of legitimation.[8] Moreover, Flanagan has seen that in each of the three pairs, there is a *rite of passage* from a more *tribal* to a distinctly *royal* world. The lists move from kinship to bureaucracy, the battle narrative is from a Philistine war to imperial wars, and the tales of legitimacy move from the ark to the dynastic oracle. Flanagan proposes that the six elements are designed and arranged to enact, in each retelling, the decisive shift *from tribe to state*. That is, they intend to

[6]Karl Budde, *Die Bücher Samuel*, Kurzer Hand-Commentar zum Alten Testament (Tübingen: J. C. B. Mohr, 1902), 304.

[7]Leonhard Rost, *The Succession to the Throne of David*, trans. David M. Gunn (Sheffield: Almond Press, 1982).

[8]James Flanagan, "Social Transformation and Ritual in 2 Samuel 6," in *The Word of the Lord Shall Go Forth*, ed. Carol M. Meyers and M. O'Connor (Winona Lake, Ind.: Eisenbrauns, 1983) 361–372. Flanagan's book, *David's Social Drama*, explicates in great detail and with great precision the thesis advanced in his article "Social Transformation and Ritual in 2 Samuel 6." Flanagan takes the text of 2 Samuel as pivotal and decisive for the larger drama of David's chiefdom.

help the listener embrace the royal ideology as the proper successor to the old tribal theory of life. Since chapters 5–8 are positive about David, it is clear that the text in these chapters means to commend royal ideology and sends David on to new power with good wishes.

When, however, we arrive at last at 2 Samuel 21, a lot has happened to David, and not much of it is good. The Succession Narrative is an artistic rendering of the failure of David's rule, a failure that pivots on the episode of Uriah and Bathsheba (2 Sam. 11–12). The narrative culminates in the pathos of beautiful, beloved Absalom being killed as an enemy of the state (2 Sam. 18:9–19:8), followed by the acrimony between north and south as they dispute who is entitled to what shares in David's success (19:11–43). It is as though the splendid propaganda machine of the throne has gone awry. The last element before the appendix is 20:23–26, a list of royal bureaucratic officials. How telling! The transformation from tribal chief to king is complete.

I believe then that chapters 21–24 are a gathering of materials to form a counterpart to the aggrandizement of absolute David, and perhaps intend to reverse the *rite of passage* in chapters 5–8 in order to provide David "passage" back into the pre-absolute world of tribal fidelity. The cumulative evidence of these chapters supports such a dismantling or deconstruction of an extravagantly royal David who has become unacceptable to the old tribal theory.[9]

A Justified Bloodbath: 2 Samuel 21:1–14. This particular narrative reports that David must kill seven sons of Saul (v. 6). The narrative presents a case in which there has been an act of bloodguilt that leads to famine and requires expiation. The initial bloodguilt that starts the entire destructive process is credited to Saul's slaughter of the Gibeonites. In an

---

[9]See Martin Cohen, "The Role of the Shilonite Priesthood in the United Monarchy of Ancient Israel," Hebrew Union College Annual 36 (1965): 59–98. On the deconstruction of royal pretensions by textual means, see Walter Brueggemann, "2 Samuel 21–24: An Appendix of Deconstruction?" *Catholic Biblical Quarterly* 50 (1988): 383–397.

attempt to save his people from the resulting famine, David must "expiate" (*kpr*) the bloodguilt by killing the sons of Saul (v. 3), thus answering the murdered blood. It may be that the narrative should be taken innocently, at face value. Even if it is taken this way, however, it is astonishing that David is portrayed as preoccupied with primitive matters of bloodguilt and ritual expiation by blood answering blood. Such a royal activity, I submit, does not fit with the high claims of bureaucratic ideology made elsewhere in the narrative but echoes a kind of primitive, prerational, pre-absolutist society.

Such an innocent reading is in my judgment, however, highly suspect. The sequence—bloodguilt, famine, and expiation—makes sense, except that there is no supporting evidence for the first act, the bloodguilt allegedly perpetrated by Saul. We have no other testimony that Saul slaughtered the Gibeonites. We would expect such a report, because the pro-David narrative wants to remember everything it can against Saul. So why no such incriminating narrative? We are permitted at least to entertain the possibility, suggested by the absence of such a narrative, that there was no such episode, no such slaughter, no such bloodguilt by Saul. The disclosure that the famine is rooted in Saul's bloodguilt is given in a private oracle to David, to which no one else has access (v. 1).

May we be so suspicious as to imagine that the "oracle" is a fabricated, contrived royal justification for David's elimination of Saul's sons who continue to threaten David? Is the narrative simply a religious excuse for a political act? If the narrative is only an excuse, we wonder what the narrative intends. If the bloodguilt of Saul is a contrivance, does the narrative believe that contrivance? Or does the narrative want us to notice the lack of supporting evidence? Is the narrative then deliberately the portrayal of a ruthless, bloodthirsty, power-hungry David who will stop at nothing to secure his throne? It could be that such an act against Saul's family is the ground for Shimei's accusation in 16:8 that David is a murderer. The narrative gives us no clue as to how it is to be read, innocently, suspiciously, or ironically. If it is read innocently, David is a mere tribal chieftain who presides over primitive religious rites. Read suspiciously, this narrative provides the rationale for a royal bloodbath. Read ironically, the narrative is in fact a massive exposé of David's ruthlessness. Read in any of these ways, the David of this narrative is not the efficient, rational, ideological king who manages a bureaucracy. The narrative works against such a sophisticated royal ideology, bespeaking a primitiveness of one kind or another.

Other Heroes: 2 Samuel 21:15–22. This list reports on four of Israel's great warriors who killed Philistine heroes. Most likely the list is primitive in its memory. In the middle of the list is a slogan of high royal theology (v. 17):

> You [David] shall no more go out with us to battle, lest you quench the lamp of Israel.

This sentiment, echoed in 18:3, shows an exaggerated view of the king's person. We might call it "high Christology." David need only *be;* he need not *do* anything.

I suggest that this high royal ideology is presented in the midst of this list in order that the ideology can be assaulted. First, in 21:15 we are told that David "grew weary." He languished in battle. But a David who grows weary in battle is not the superhuman agent suggested by the slogan of verse 17. He is one who is subject to the pressures of human reality. The narrative nicely places in tension the high slogan of verse 17 with the realism of verse 15.

Moreover, in 21:19 it is reported that Elhanan killed Goliath. In terms of historical investigation, it is unclear whether David or Elhanan killed Goliath or whether the two names somehow refer to the same man. Our problem here, however, is not a historical problem of who killed Goliath. Rather we ask, what did the narrative intend by this notation about Elhanan? It is plausible that Elhanan had in fact killed Goliath, and in the great narrative of 1 Samuel 17 that victory is reassigned by the tradition to David. If that is the case, then the present notation clearly intends to debunk David by taking the victory away from David and reassigning it to Elhanan. Such a narrative procedure robs David of yet another public claim. Other Israelite heroes seem to manage against the Philistines very well without David.

I suggest that the ideological claim of 2 Samuel 21:17 is made empty and ludicrous by being placed between the note on David's weariness and the claim of Elhanan. David is portrayed as ineffective and irrelevant in the struggle with the Philistines. In the main story of the books of Samuel, David is preeminently successful against the Philistines. Here, however, Israelite success against the Philistines is accomplished without any specific claim for David. The irrelevance of David gives the lie to pretentious royal theology. In this brief passage, Israel is shown to be not at all in need of David.

Retribution from a Doxological "Thou": 2 Samuel 22:1–51. This long poem existed independently before it was placed in this particular location. Its use as an independent poem is evident in Psalm 18. Thus it is highly probable that a free-standing poem has been appropriated for use in our narrative. The psalm falls into three parts.

First, 22:1–20 is a *song of deliverance.* The singer acknowledges that God has rescued him from dire straits. Verses 2–4 are an initial acknowledgment of Yahweh's rescue with a torrent of words that characterize God's protection: rock, fortress, refuge, shield, horn, stronghold, and then three uses of the verb "save." Verses 5–6 utilize high mythic language about the "waves of death," "the torrents of perdition, the cords of Sheol." These images concern being drawn down into the waters of chaos before which the speaker is completely helpless. In verses 8–20, conventional language of theophany is used to characterize the powerful coming of Yahweh. The language is a counter and response to the imagery of vs. 5–6. It describes the disruption when God comes, causing the earth to rock and reel. God rides on a cherub, with clouds for a canopy, there is thunder and lightning. This powerful God reaches down into the waters and rescues (v. 18). God is shown to be powerful and wondrously reliable.

The entire poem thus far is completely focused on God.

The speaker scarcely appears, except as a voice of need. In the midst of this powerful mythic language, 22:7 contains a simple covenantal statement, "I cried, God heard." The speaker is a helpless suppliant. The poem, the speaker, the flood are all dominated by the coming of God who changes everything.

The final element of the poem (22:29–51) is *a victory song*. In contrast to the initial song of deliverance, the victory song permits the speaker, presumably David, to assert all that he has done to defeat his enemies:

> I can crush a troop,
> I can leap over a wall (v. 30),
> I pursued my enemies,
> I destroyed them,
> I consumed them,
> I thrust them through (vs. 38–39),
> I beat them fine,
> I crushed them,
> I stamped them down (v. 43).

These verbs in the victory song allow the royal voice to celebrate and congratulate himself. The extended self-assertion is matched, however, perhaps overmatched, by the "Thou" statements referring to God. Even the victory song asserts that it is the power and fidelity of Yahweh which is decisive. The power of the royal speaker is subordinated to and derived from the power of Yahweh. Finally the claim of the king ends in praise of and yielding to Yahweh. The king dramatically yields to the real governance of Yahweh (22:50–51):

> For this I will extol thee, O LORD,
>   among the nations,
>   and sing praises to thy name.
> Great triumphs he gives to his king,
>   and shows steadfast love to his anointed,
>   to David, and his descendants for ever.

Everything depends on Yahweh's steadfast love. It is Yahweh's fidelity which lies behind Yahweh's powerful intervention (22:36–41):

> *Thou* hast given me the shield of thy salvation,
> 　and *thy* help made me great.
> *Thou* didst give a wide place
> 　for my steps under me, . . .
> For *thou* didst gird me with strength for the battle;
> 　*thou* didst make my assailants sink under me.
> *Thou* didst make my enemies turn their backs to me.

In 22:7, Yahweh answers the speaker who calls. This has its negative counterpart in verse 42:

> They cried to the LORD,
> 　but he did not answer them.

In the end, everything depends on Yahweh's answer. If Yahweh answers, there is life. If Yahweh does not answer, there is only death.

Between the *song of rescue* (2 Sam. 22:1–20) and the *song of victory* (vs. 29–51) is the middle portion, verses 21–28. This section, in contrast to the two doxological sections, is didactic. It speaks of *moral symmetry and strict retribution.* God rewards according to righteousness and wickedness. The speaker dares to affirm (vs. 21–26):

> The LORD rewarded [*gml*] me
> 　according to my righteousness;
> 　according to the cleanness of my hands
> 　　he recompensed me [*šûb*].
> For I have kept the ways of the LORD,
> 　and have not wickedly departed from my God. . . .
> I did not turn aside.
> I was blameless [*tmm*] before him,
> And I kept myself from guilt.
> Therefore the LORD has recompensed me [*šûb*]
> 　according to my righteousness,
> 　according to my cleanness in his sight. . . .
> With the blameless man [*tmm*] thou dost show
> 　thyself blameless.

The language is not unlike that of 1 Samuel 26:23, in which David asserts his own righteousness. There is an important difference, however. The claim of the earlier passage is an-

ticipatory of the coming story of David. The critical point of
the David narrative is still to come. The narrator and the
voice of David can still posture innocence. Now, however,
in this poem placed at the end of the David story, this assertion is made after David's story has played itself out. We
know the sordid details that have filled out the story. The
high claims of innocence, virtue, and merit now seem less
than convincing and do not ring true.

Either this daring statement is high royal theology for a
righteous king,[10] that is to say, an ideological claim in spite
of the data, or it is an ironic statement. I suggest it is the
latter in its present location. Israel knew better than to celebrate such a "cleaned up" David. In 1 Kings 15:4, in
another reference to a "royal lamp" in Israel, the Deuteronomist has given a most telling verdict on David: "David did
what was right in the eyes of the LORD, and did not turn
aside from anything that he commanded him all the days of
his life—except in the matter of Uriah the Hittite." "Except" indeed! This is a massive exception. Moreover, the
narrative of exception (2 Sam. 11–12) is known in Israel and
cannot be overlooked.

This candid acknowledgment in 1 Kings 15:5 poses a dilemma concerning how to relate the reality of David's life to
the high claims of retribution theology in these verses. I
think the poet is fully aware of the narrative of David and
intends the reader to be fully aware as well. It is known in
Israel that David is not marked by *ṣedaqah* (righteousness)
and is not *tamîm* (perfect). The real David is known in Israel
and will not be denied, even by the robust singing of this
hymn. While the middle section of this song (2 Sam. 22:21–
28) seems innocently to credit David's success to his virtue,
the other two sections of the psalm (vs. 1–20, 29–51) know
better. The deliverance in the first part of the poem is
clearly Yahweh's free, massive gift. The victory celebrated at
the end of the poem finally submits royal claims to the deci-

---

[10]See Brevard S. Childs, *Introduction to the Old Testament as Scripture*
(Philadelphia: Fortress Press, 1979), 273–275.

sive "Thou" of Yahweh. The well-being of David thus is not a reward for virtue; rather, it is the free gift of Yahweh, given even in the face of David's sin. The opening and closing parts of the psalm require that the middle section (which appears so innocent) be read critically and ironically.

The outcome of such a three-part juxtaposition is that the king who might wish to claim virtue and achievement for himself is like every other Israelite. He is only an empty-handed suppliant before Yahweh, totally dependent on Yahweh's willingness to listen and to answer and intervene. The king's own person and career have in fact achieved nothing, guaranteed nothing, and deserved nothing. It is Yahweh, always Yahweh, only Yahweh who delivers. It is all Yahweh, no one else, surely not the king.

Read in this context, the middle section of the poem sounds very different. In fact it does not celebrate the king as it first appears, but it indicts the king and shows how the known realities of David's life require a God who hears willingly and acts freely. This middle section firmly nullifies any pretension that the king has merit, authority, or legitimacy of his own from which to make demands on God.

This psalm, which ostensibly celebrates royal ideology, when placed in its present context, undermines such ideology and resubmits the king to the old covenantal practice of "cry–hear." The king is a suppliant before Yahweh. That is not a new role especially assigned to the king, for a suppliant is what Israel has always been.

A Covenant Based in Righteousness: 2 Samuel 23:1–7. This psalm undoubtedly voices high royal theology. In verse 1 David is one who is "raised on high" and "anointed," and in verse 2 it is the "spirit of Yahweh" who has authorized kingship. This high claim is matched in verse 5, where the king asserts:

> For he has made with me an everlasting covenant,
> ordered in all things and secure.

The phrase, "everlasting covenant" (*berît 'ôlam*) surely echoes the central ideological decree of 2 Sam. 7:14–16, which

reverberates in Psalm 89:24, 33–36. God's guarantee of the
monarchy is unconditional and therefore perpetual.

How odd, however, that between 23:1–2 and 23:5, both
of which make high claims for the monarchy, a crucial motif
is introduced that moves against such absolutist ideology (vs.
3b–4):

> When one rules justly (*ṣaddîq*) over men,
>   ruling in the fear of God,
> [then] he dawns on them like the morning light,
>   like the sun shining forth upon a cloudless
>   morning,
>   like rain that makes grass to sprout from the
>   earth.

The king is like light, like sun, like rain, i.e., the king is
indeed the giver of life! That role of the king, however, is
premised on *ṣaddîq*, on doing righteously. The king is not
automatically, unreservedly the source of life, but only
where the king rules according to the torah.[11]

I am not suggesting that this psalm is consistently critical
of royal theology. It does, however, articulate a wondrous
tension. It is this middle element (23:3b–4) that challenges
the exaggerated claims at the beginning and end of the
poem. The conditionality of *ṣaddîq* warns against every easy
royal claim. It is the old covenant tradition that insists upon
and sounds the "if" of obedience, the conditionality of justice, the critical reservation of covenantal practice.

This central, teasing verse thus echoes the conditionality
so powerfully articulated by Samuel himself, who is endlessly suspicious of royal ideology. Samuel warned Israel:

> If you will fear the LORD and serve him and harken to his voice
> and not rebel, . . . if *both you and your king* who reigns over
> you . . . , it will be well. But if you will not hearken . . . , then

---

[11]The tension between vs. 1–2, 5 and v. 3 has the same structure as
Psalm 72, in which vs. 1–4, 12–14 speak of royal responsibility and vs. 5–
11, 15–17 speak of royal power and splendor. Psalm 72 does not explicitly
make the power of the king conditional on responsibility as in our poem,
but the implication seems clearly to be the same.

the hand of the LORD will be against *you and your king*. . . .
But if you still do wickedly, you shall be swept away, *both you
and your king.*

(1 Samuel 12:14–15, 25)

Three times in the warning there is the ominous phrase,
"You and your king." The king is not different from every
other Israelite. The king is "like you," like all Israelites,
subject to the same norms and expectations, exposed to the
same jeopardy. It turns out that the *berît* is not *'ad 'ôlam;*
the covenant is not forever. Rather, the covenant is for as
long as the rule of the king is just and power is administered
covenantally. Thus one should not place too much confi-
dence in the high claims of royal theology.

This conditionality in 23:3 is the same as operates in Nathan's rebuke of David after the Uriah-Bathsheba incident.
In 1 Kings 2:2–4, moreover, the same "if" is placed in the
mouth of David by the Deuteronomist. In 2 Sam. 23:1–7,
the royal ideology is not silenced, but it is severely re-
stricted and critiqued. Thus in both poems of the appendix,
we have a crafted, cunning artistry that does indeed celebrate royal theology, but at the same time warns against its
own overstated claims. The royal claim is both made and
qualified in the same poetry. This playful unresolve likely
reflects exactly how Israel at its most alert must have
thought about this enduring tension of torah and king.

A New Brand of Greatness: 2 Samuel 23:8–39. The second
list in the appendix consists in two lists of heroes, "the
Three" and "the Thirty." These are the great ones of military courage and prowess who are named on the special days
of remembrance. This is early Israel's Hall of Fame. I make
only four comments on this list.

1. The list evidences a remarkable democratic tendency.
There are many heroes in early premonarchic Israel. The
exploits of many are known and remembered. Their names
are precious and visible. David did not need to have a monopoly on greatness and public acclamation. Such a democratizing tendency clearly works against high royal theology.

In the personality cult of absolutist kings, there can be no
other heroes. No names can be honored except that of the
king, who preempts all other claims and monopolizes all
great exploits. In this list the power is still shared, the glory
is spread around. Indeed, in this list David does not do anything and is not celebrated for his prowess or courage.
While not an exact counterpart, this inclusive list suggests
that David is not jealous as was Saul in 1 Samuel 18:7–8,
when Saul was enraged that the women named David as well
as himself. This list suggests an openness on the part of royal
theology, without defensiveness.

2. In 2 Samuel 23:10, 12, the victories reported are credited to Yahweh: "The LORD wrought a great victory that
day." The list has a theonomous cast in which Yahweh is
reckoned to be the key and decisive actor. In the formula of
vs. 10, 12, David is not even mentioned, suggesting that the
list knows David is marginal to Israel's well-being. In 2 Samuel 8:6, 14, it is said that Yahweh gave David victory, and in
8:13 David "wins a name for himself." But not here. In this
list David needs no such emphasis and receives none. The
theonomous cast of the narrative, which severely relativizes
David, is the counterpart to the democratizing tendency already noted. The theonomous and democratizing tendencies
both work critically against high royal theology.

3. The last name among the thirty is "Uriah the Hittite" (2
Sam. 23:39). It may be routine that Uriah's name is in-
cluded. Perhaps his name belonged there on its merit. It
cannot be routine or accidental, however, that his name is
last. Uriah's name is last as a gesture, a reminder, a warning,
a daring underscoring. When the recital of great names is
ended, the name of Uriah continues to echo in the ears of
Israel. The echo evokes the sordidness of 2 Samuel 11,
which is no more forgotten than is Chappaquiddick. Not everything needs to be said explicitly. Some things need only
to be hinted at or suggested.

The ominousness of the phrase, "Uriah the Hittite,"
grows with every sounding of it. The list asserts, against all
royal pretensions, "We have not forgotten." What we remember is the crucial scenario of royal arrogance, pride,

autonomy, and brutality, when for an instant, the king forgot the claims of torah and imagined he stood free of torah. We also have not forgotten the chastening indictment of Nathan (2 Sam. 12:7), the repentance and brokenness of David (12:13), and Nathan's terrible ordination of a sword of curse suspended tenuously over the dynasty (12:10). The presence of Uriah in the list reminds Israel that beyond the king and his extravagant claims, there is another governance that will not be mocked, harnessed, or preempted. What is "pleasing in the eyes" of the king does not necessarily please "the eyes of Yahweh" (cf. 2 Sam. 11:25, 27). This list serves as more than a general statement of theonomy or of democracy. It is the mobilization and enactment of a quite specific memory that constitutes Israel's foundational criticism of royal ideology. The list is a daring footnote that makes the royal pretension enormously fragile.

4. In the middle of this peculiar list is an odd, poignant narrative (2 Sam. 23:13–17). It records David's wish for water from Bethlehem, while he is in the midst of the Philistine battle. His word is more a wish than a request, certainly not a command. Because his men so adore him and are eager to obey his wish, they secure water from Bethlehem at the risk of their lives. They are pleased with themselves. They anticipate David's satisfaction with them and his commendation of them. David, however, is always beyond our prediction. In a magnificent gesture of solidarity, in an act of "sacramental imagination," David pours the hard-gained water on the ground.[12] He says, "Shall I drink the blood of the men who went at risk of their lives?" (v. 17). His men must have adored him all the more and been ready to obey him in every whim and wish.

Certainly the story intends to enhance further the greatness of David. The story, however, focuses on and aims at a very peculiar notion of greatness. This is not the greatness of magnificence and splendor reflecting absolutism. This David

[12]For the notion of "sacramental imagination," see Jack L. Seymour et. al., *The Church in the Education of the Public* (Nashville: Abingdon Press, 1984), 134–153.

has not remained back in the royal palace (contra 2 Sam. 11:1; 18:3–4; 21:17) but is at risk with his comrades in battle. The narrative is about the greatness of David's solidarity with his fighting men. Moreover David is a man with a need, or at least an unsatisfied desire. Those with him are his comrades, not his servants. David does not treat the men as servants, and the narrator does not present them as such.

The most important point, of course, is that David does not drink the water. David does not assume he is entitled to benefit from the service and risk of his comrades. David does not claim a disproportionate benefit, certainly not a monopoly. In high royal theology, the king characteristically is assigned a disproportionate share of what is good, if not a monopoly. David, however, eschews such preferential status and acts in solidarity. David clearly has great power over the mighty men. His power is, however, the power of magisterial humanness, not ideological priority or bureaucratic leverage. This brief narrative is a portrayal of the greatness of David that the narrator commends. It is not the greatness of bureaucratic absoluteness nor of dominance on the battlefield. It is rather the greatness of one "among the brothers" (cf. Deut. 17:15), not seeking advantage or promoting special status for himself.

This episode in the midst of the list of "the Three" and "the Thirty" presents David in the midst of the conflict and risk of life. No doubt David commands respect among the soldiers. The others, however, are "the great ones." David's preeminence is not formal and not imposed, but emerges from his willingness to be in solidarity. The narrative models a brand of greatness very different from high royal pretension (cf. Mark 10:42–43).

Counting, but Only on Mercy: 2 Samuel 24:1–25. Finally we come to the second narrative in the appendix, a most curious narrative. It begins in 24:1 with the assertion that Yahweh was angry at Israel and "incited" David against Israel. The narrative begins with the strange suggestion that it is king *against* people. Yahweh evokes in David a resolve to conduct a census of Judah.

Verse 1 lies outside David's awareness and outside the action of the narrative plot. It asserts that more is going on in David's rule than David knows or administers. Indeed, the verse asserts that David is not the key actor in his own career, though no doubt he thought he was. It asserts, moreover, that a royal census is not a neutral tool of policy, as no doubt David thought it was, but is in fact an act of judgment against Israel, given only because Yahweh is angry. In this first verse there is enormous narrative suggestiveness and freighted theological intentionality that is not obvious, either to David or to us. An act of state policy is presented as an enactment of Yahweh's anger. We are given no reason for that anger. Yahweh's anger is the first "given" of the narrative. In verse 2, we are told simply that David proceeds to implement the census. There is an odd, silent gap between verses 1 and 2. David is obedient to Yahweh's "inciting." David's readiness to conduct a census also suggests the play of power and royal ideology that are now in the purview and perhaps the habit of David.

The instigation of Yahweh (24:1) and the proposal of David (v. 2) are strongly resisted by Joab (v. 3). Joab is the crusty voice of the old tradition. The narrator uses the voice of Joab against the novel state policy of David. Joab, however, does not persuade David. How could he, against the political resolve of David when coupled with the hidden initiative of Yahweh! The execution of the census is given in considerable detail (vs. 4–9). The characterization of the census bespeaks administrative flurry, fast horses, ruthless officers, high-minded, insensitive bureaucrats, government agents charging into obscure, unresponsive villages. The census is a form of bureaucratic terrorism in which the crown invades village and tribal life. The royal intrusion violates village separateness, disrupts community, and seeks to mobilize the resources of the village and tribe for purposes that are of indifference to the village and tribe. Censuses serve only royal administration and deployment, not the villages themselves.

In 24:9 we learn the purpose of David's census. There are "800,000 valiant men who draw the sword." This is the king counting the cost before he goes to battle (cf. Luke 14:28). Indeed, beyond our contemporary passion for market research, a census can only serve two purposes. One purpose is taxation, the other is the military draft. David is on his way to mobilizing indifferent, unresponsive villages for his own power, his own expansive ambition, his own self-aggrandizing ends. David is now prepared to "take," as Samuel had anticipated in 1 Samuel 8:11–18. This is royal policy in all its unattractive, alienating character. The census shifts the fundamental presuppositions of public life.

Abruptly, upon completion of the census, David asserts, "I have sinned . . . I have done very foolishly" (24:10). We do not know how David came to this awareness of his sin. It is as though David "came to himself," like a prodigal coming home. In this narrative, David has enough critical distance from his ambitious policy to identify the dangerous seductiveness of royal ideology.[13]

David's response in his new awareness is to pray. His confession and prayer enact a complete reversal, a complete break with the ideology of autonomy he has just been implementing. In this moment of religious submissiveness, David is no longer the ambitious servant of self-sufficiency. He is back in touch with the demanding realities of torah religion.

Through the mediation of Gad the prophet, David is permitted to choose between three punishments: famine, war, and pestilence (24:11–13). David must choose from among the classical possibilities. We are not told why choices are given. The offer of options belongs to the playfulness of the narrative. David's response is wondrous. David evidences a theological suppleness and responsiveness we would not

---

[13]In this text, David has the remarkable and inexplicable capacity to be aware on his own of his violation of torah. This is unlike 2 Samuel 12, where his self-deception is much greater. In ch. 12, the persuasive, weighty confrontation of Nathan is required to make the point of David's guilt. This contrast between chapters 12 and 24 suggests that the David offered in the appendices is much more open to the old covenantal traditions that these chapters advocate.

have anticipated in vs. 1–4. David responds to Gad: "I am in great distress; let us fall into the hand of the LORD, for his mercy is great; but let me not fall into the hand of man" (v. 14). At the outset of the narrative David had imagined himself free to do what he wanted to do. He is a man who does not reckon with Yahweh and does not reckon on Yahweh. He can manage.

At this crucial turn in the narrative, we are offered a very different David. After 24:10, David is no longer the one who is autonomous and can manage. Now he is a responsive king. The difference is that he has reentered the sphere of Yahweh's rule. He enters that sphere through his acknowledgment of his own failure. The overriding new reality, however, is not David's recognition of his own failure but his acknowledgment of Yahweh's mercy. It is the mercy of Yahweh that now becomes decisive for the narrative, a mercy not previously articulated in this narrative and not acknowledged previously in this narrative by David. The story turns at verse 10 because of new articulations of both David and Yahweh. David will receive mercy from Yahweh which he does not expect from any human transaction. It is David's trust in Yahweh in this narrative, his new trust in Yahweh, which dictates David's choice of punishment.

The narrative exhibits another element of playfulness. Yahweh is merciful, but not quickly or easily. The whole land is smitten with the pestilence (24:15). The angel of death moves freely and coldly. When the angel moves against Jerusalem, however, after 70,000 deaths, then Yahweh recalls the angel (v. 16). The holy city, David's city, is spared. In the end, Yahweh is merciful.[14] Yahweh will not permit death to have its final say against the city of David, for the final say of Yahweh toward David is mercy.

The massive death for which David is responsible, and for which he knows he is responsible, drives him to reiterate the

---

[14]There are, to be sure, many difficult questions about divine justice in this narrative. The narrator, however, brackets out all such questions. He does not address them or even acknowledge that such questions are present in the story.

confession of 24:10 in verse 17. In the earlier verse, the double confession was:

> I have sinned greatly . . . ,
> I have done exceedingly foolishly.

The adverb *me'od*, "exceedingly," is used twice to make the confession intense. In verse 17, the double confession is different:

> I have sinned . . .
> I have done wickedly.

The adverb of intensification (*me'od*) has been dropped. But the following petition is also changed. In verse 10, David prayed for himself. Now, however, in verse 17, David gets beyond himself and prays for his people, for the ones against whom in verse 1, Yahweh had the initial anger:

> But these sheep, what have they done? Let thy hand, I pray thee, be against me and against my father's house.

This is prayer at its most mature. David knows he is guilty. He petitions that the fully deserved punishment (which he does not challenge) should be focused on him and his family, and should not spill over on his innocent realm. In this prayer of petition, David makes a decisive break with royal ideology and understands that it is the kingdom and not the king which is finally important.[15]

In 24:18–25a, there is a long narrative interlude that perhaps was originally an aetiological tale, i.e., a story designed to explain the cause of something. Those verses tell how David buys an adequate place for a sacrifice and then offers the sacrifice. That is, they explain how the later temple site

---

[15]David's passionate petition in v. 17 makes a sharp contrast with the royal ideology critiqued in Ezekiel 34. In that chapter, kings (shepherds) are condemned because they were uninterested in the welfare of the sheep and were willing to exploit the sheep endlessly for their own well-being. Quite in contrast, David seeks to protect the sheep, i.e., the governed community, and petitions that the deserved punishment should be focused only on him and on his house. The narrative has David break with self-serving royal practice.

is rooted in David's purchase. The narrative ends with a resolution (v 25b):

> So Yahweh heeded supplications for the land, and the plague
> was averted from Israel.

Verse 25 has an odd but direct link to verse 1, where Yahweh is angry with Israel. Now in verse 25, the anger of Yahweh against Israel is turned away, because of David's sacrifice and prayer. David has become a king who deals with Yahweh on covenantal terms. The narrative enacts a remarkable transformation of David, a "deconstruction" of a census-taking absolutist. The arrogant, self-serving king who initiates a census now throws himself on God's mercy, to petition for his people. In the end, David saves the very people he had sought to exploit by the census. Through the narrative, David has been returned to a proper covenantal mode of life from which he had been seduced by royal ideology and by the "inciting" of Yahweh.

A Literary Subversion of Excessive Claims

The appendix of 2 Samuel 21–24 is a remarkable, subtle, and intentional literary unity built out of preexisting, independent literary traditions. Taken together, these materials suggest a subtle subversion of royal pretension; a debunking of excessive ideology that has taken the form of pride, autonomy, and self-sufficiency; and an assertion that true kingship has to do with honoring covenantal responsibilities and obeying the will of the God of the Mosaic tradition. The narrative does not simply report these matters but in fact enacts that which it advocates. It makes palpable in Israel the dramatic sequence by which an arrogant, self-serving king is brought back to the realities of Yahweh from which he came. Each time Israel hears these narratives, it again participates in the drama of dismantling whereby royal power is again embedded in the powerful truth of torah religion. My reading suggests the following comments.

1. *In the two narratives:*
    a. In 21:1–14 on the expiation of bloodguilt, David is presented either as a child of extreme religious scruple who attends to a genuinely religious crisis, or as a bloodthirsty practitioner of *Realpolitik*. In either case, this David is not the grand bureaucratic monarch but the one who attends to hidden forces he cannot manage or even understand. The issues of this text are not the matters out of which great worldly power is formed and consolidated.
    b. In 24:1–25 David is transformed from a self-serving bureaucratic monarch to a repentant suppliant who relies on and receives the mercy of Yahweh. David in this narrative is redescribed in intentional theological categories.
2. *In the two lists,* David is portrayed as a leader who has power in the context of other faithful, loyal persons whom he does not control or even sponsor.
    a. In 21:15–21 there is a high claim of royal theology (in v. 17), but it is encompassed in statements of weariness and inactivity. The king does not dominate or enact the courage and effectiveness of Israel.
    b. In 23:8–39 David is set in a horizon of theonomous, democratic practice. David is portrayed as a comrade in solidarity, not as a king who dominates.
3. *In the two songs,* there is indeed celebration of high royal theology. In both poems, however, that high claim is critiqued and qualified.
    a. In 22:1–51 the celebration of the king is qualified by the massive claim of Yahweh's initiative, and by the awareness that the self-announcement of royal righteousness and cleanness (given what we know of David) cannot be the ground of Yahweh's rescue and care.
    b. In 23:1–7 the high assertion of an "eternal covenant" is placed in jeopardy by the awareness that the covenant depends on the doing of *ṣedaqah* by the king.

By the finish of this set of texts in the appendix, David no longer sounds so much like a brutal despot, nor even like "Solomon in all his glory." Indeed, David sounds much more like Hannah, vulnerable, vexed, and barren, who made supplication and was heard (1 Sam. 1:9–28), than like Solomon, who is not vulnerable or vexed. When God hears Hannah's prayer, Hannah sings songs of praise to the one who "raises up the poor from the dust . . . to make them sit with princes" (1 Sam. 2:6–8). In the end, David is like Hannah.[16] David's main royal work in 2 Samuel 24 is to petition for mercy. As the tale ends, Yahweh hears the supplication and saves Israel (2 Sam. 24:25). In his acts of confession, petition, and repentance, David is made freshly aware of the God who raises the lowly to sit with princes. David may thus sing out of his vulnerability. He may again sit with princes, but for now he will remember that he is from among the poor and therefore may be amazed, grateful, and dependent.[17] Such a David is equipped, at least for a time, to resist the threat and seduction of royal ideology.

A Passage Back to Faith, Wrought in Narrative

This exposition of 2 Samuel 21–24, informed by Flanagan's work on 2 Samuel 5–8, has related the text to *rites of passage*. The rite of passage here proposed and enacted by the text wants to destabilize and delegitimate the powerful, pretentious David of the main story. That David had grown self-sufficient and unresponsive. He seemed to have no need

[16]On the textual-dramatic relation of Hannah and David, see Walter Brueggemann, "I Samuel 1: A Sense of a Beginning," *Zeitschrift für die alttestamentliche Wissenschaft* 102 (1990), 33–48.

[17]David is not unlike Nebuchadnezzar in Daniel 4. Through a hard chastening, Nebuchadnezzar had learned that he does not hold power by special privilege, merit, or right, but that Yahweh gives power "to whomever he will." In his transformed situation, David seems to learn the same hard reality. The narratives of both David and Nebuchadnezzar articulate a key biblical insistence about power, namely, that power is held only as a gift and free grant from Yahweh. Outside that free grant of Yahweh, the king has no claim or power, either in Israel or in Babylon.

for his fellows and no need for Yahweh. He had sufficient resources to make his own way. This practical self-sufficiency was matched by a royal theology that moved in the direction of kingship as an indispensable structure in Israel. This narrative in 2 Samuel 21–24 moves dramatically against such a notion of autonomous, self-sufficient power. These texts in the appendix intend to expose such pretense as untenable, and, out of an older critical tradition, to sketch another way of royal power. Both the critical exposé of royal pretension and the alternative sketch of covenantal possibility are accomplished with subtle artistry. These texts take up old traditional pieces of material, perhaps fashioning some new ones, and placing them in a careful arrangement to lead to the conclusion of 24:25. In that last verse, David is an empty-handed suppliant. In that condition, however, David is heard and Israel saved.

Liturgy as an Arena for Reimagined Life

It is an easy step from these narrative rites of passage to enquire about liturgy, and how these texts may invite us to notice the risk and prospect of liturgy. Worship is aimed at the glory of God. We worship precisely that God may be glorified. Sociologists and anthropologists, however, have noticed that the latent work and by-product of public worship is more than and other than its acknowledged theological work. That is, liturgy not only glorifies God; it also constructs a community and produces structures of plausibility for the community.[18] Such liturgical work is never explicit, direct, or immediately visible; it can, however, be done with intentionality. These texts as rites of passage (chapters 5–8 from tribal chieftain to royal figure, and chapters 21–24 from royal figure back to tribal chieftain) suggest that liturgy and its textual articulation serve to enact models of power and legitimacy. As these texts both legitimate and

[18]On liturgy as world-construction, see Walter Brueggemann, *Israel's Praise: Doxology Against Idolatry and Ideology* (Philadelphia: Fortress Press, 1988), chapter 1.

dismantle a certain kind of David (and with him a certain perception of power), so our liturgy and its text serve both to legitimate and to dismantle certain kinds of power.

Insofar as my analysis of chapters 21–24 is correct, the chapters suggest to me a "liturgical" enactment of the transformation of power to vulnerability, of fullness to emptiness, of pretension to fidelity.[19] By its capacity to propose, mediate, and enact alternative modes of life, liturgy may serve to dismantle and delegitimate pretentious forms of power that are autonomous and self-sufficient, inviting to an alternative mode of community that casts itself, like Hannah and David, on the mercy of God. Liturgy may function to transform the community back to simple trust in the power and mercy of God.

This narrative is a model of the way in which the Bible reimagines life. These narratives show David being reimagined. I have no doubt that a major enterprise in our contemporary situation is to reimagine life away from old configurations of power to new public possibilities. When one asks where such reimagining of public possibility might happen, the most realistic answer is the liturgy. The liturgy in any event is an act of imagination. In churches allied with the status quo as custodians for present power arrangements, the imaginative action of liturgy is reiterative and reproductive of what already is.

In churches where there is an energized sense that God is calling us to newness that impinges on public power, then

---

[19]The movement in this direction from fullness to emptiness applies only to chapters 21–24. The movement in chapters 5–8 is in the other direction, from emptiness to fullness. In some interpretive contexts, among the marginalized and disadvantaged, chapters 5–8 may be the more appropriate text and are perhaps a better clue to the urgent responsibility of liturgy. I make my argument from chapters 21–24 in the context of mainline U.S. churches which are historically "full" and are, in my judgment, now summoned to leanness. The different liturgical functions of "filling" and "emptying" as respectively authorized by chapters 5–8 and 21–24 correlate with what James A. Sanders, *From Sacred Story to Sacred Text* (Philadelphia: Fortress Press, 1987), 67–68, has termed "prophetic" (critical) and "constitutive" hermeneutics.

the liturgy is not reproductive of what is, but productive of something utterly new. Then the liturgy is not reiterative of what is known but asserts what has not been. My judgment is that Christian liturgy, when freed by the spirit and informed by the gospel, tends to be productive of newness. The best examples of this, of course, occur in communities under oppression where the reception of God's promises for rescue and emancipation cause the liturgy to subvert all settled conventions of public reality. I wish in these comments to connect two matters. On the one hand, these David narratives are acts of such imaginative subversion. On the other hand, such acts of imaginative subversion are indeed urgent for our time and place. It is instructive and telling that in the recent emancipation of Eastern Europe, the church played a crucial role as a meeting place for alternative, imaginative scenarios of public reality. The imaginative acts unleashed enormous power in the play of governance. I suggest these narratives model the same intention.

I pursue this point because I believe that the mainline (or old-line) U.S. churches at worship are in a situation comparable to David's new pretension in the royal establishment of Jerusalem, excessively full of themselves. What is needed now, as then, for fidelity and indeed for survival, is a relinquishment of false perceptions of reality that are excessively self-congratulatory. The glory of God is a counter to the glory of Solomon. The glorification of God holds out the promise of a relinquishment of royal claims.

The texts invite those with power, and with presumed absolute power, to imagine and conceptualize their lives differently, i.e., without such pretensions to absolutism. As David and Solomon and their ilk are addressed in ancient Israel, so the texts might derivatively address us in our presumed absolute power.

At least four dimensions of relinquishment might belong to our return to another mode of life and faith. Whenever such relinquishment is embraced, we discover that the capacity to relinquish is in fact a miracle of transformation. What we had perceived as loss turns out to be a miracle of liberation. So David relinquished royal pretension and was liberated for God's attentive mercy. In our situation, a relinquishment of idolatrous self-sufficiency can liberate to new covenantal humanity. These dimensions are peculiarly poignant in our situation, but are not unlike those faced in ancient Israel whenever there were pretensions to absoluteness and self-sufficiency:

1. False and destructive reliance on *massive military power.*
2. False and destructive devotion to our *excessive standard of living* in a world of betrayed economics.
3. False and destructive *images of self* in various psychologies of self-actualization that screen out issues of justice.
4. False and destructive *notions of certitude,* political, moral, and theological, that work toward control rather than yielding fidelity.[20]

The costly relinquishment required for covenantalism does not address us all equally; the requirement of transformation addresses whites more than blacks and other racial minorities, males more than females, urban patterns of power more than rural. All of us, however, are children of a Western ideology that echoes the dangers of royal Jerusalem.[21] I am making an interpretive linkage between

---

[20]All these dimensions of dismantling are interrelated; together they embody a bloated sense of self-importance and an unspoken assumption that we are entitled to a disproportionate share of everything. Paul Kennedy, *The Rise and Fall of the Great Powers: Economic Change and Military Conflict from 1500 to 2000* (New York: Random House, 1987), 531–535, suggests that "Great Powers" must eventually return to their "natural share" of resources related to their "natural size." The several dismantlings now faced in U.S. society represent exactly such a task of returning to "natural share" in terms of military, economic, and political power and the religious-cultural self-perceptions that accompany these modes of power. See "Note and Comments," *The New Yorker* (May 8, 1989), 31–32, for a helpful comment on Kennedy's thesis. I suggest that our task of returning to "natural share" is not unlike the task urged in 2 Sam. 21–24 for a royal Israel that overestimated its size and overreached its share.

[21]On costly relinquishment as now required of the "full ones" in the world, see Marie Augusta Neal, *A Socio-Theology of Letting Go: The Role*

"royal Jerusalem" and our dominant "Western ideology."
Such an interpretive connection is not obvious, but it
seems to me fair and credible. By Western ideology I mean
the dominant values of the Enlightenment, which include
commitments to autonomy, individualism, and self-sufficiency. Those commitments get expressed in terms of an
epistemology of positivism and in an economics of greed
and affluence. Those commitments are deep within the fab-
ric of our common life and touch us all, liberal and conservative. I suggest that those values, mutatis mutandis, are
the ones that seduced David into the pursuit of power and
security in ways that nearly destroyed him and that were
to reach their apex in the reign of Solomon.

It is against that convergence of temptations that the texts
of 2 Samuel 21–24 protest. That sequence is a daring literary achievement. It tells dangerous tales and sings dangerous songs in the very face of royal power. It asks each
generation of the royal entourage to imagine what it would
be like to be full, and then not to think too highly of ourselves (Rom. 12:3). It imagines a monarchy that has become
empty for the sake of obedience, even to forms of death, and
then to be exalted by the one who raises the needy from the
ash heap to sit with princes (cf. Phil. 2:9–11).[22]

---

of a First World Church Facing Third World Peoples (New York: Paulist
Press, 1977), and *The Just Demands of the Poor* (New York: Paulist Press,
1987). I would not want to press the parallelism excessively, but a case
can be made that the premonarchic Israel which produced David was a
third-world people, who under Solomon became "developed," something like a first-world people. Such a labeling is of course anachronistic;
it nonetheless illuminates the point I am making about the intention of
chapters 21–24, and about the potential of liturgy.

[22]In his poignant novel *Rumors of Rain* (London: W. H. Allen, 1978), 69–
70, André Brink has Charlie, the African, quote to Martin, the Afrikaner,
the warning about gaining the world and losing your soul:

" 'There's one thing you forgot, Martin.'

'What's that?'

'Morality.'

'What's morality?'

'A matter of conscience. I'm just as bad a believer as you are. But on
Bernard's farm, where he and I grew up, the *oubaas'*—I'm sure he said that

Liturgy is indeed serious, dangerous business. Liturgy is the primary place in our regularized life of power, control, and self-sufficiency where we engage old alternative memories and we are invited home.

deliberately—'the *oubaas* loved to read us the text about gaining the world and losing your soul. Don't you think that's where you should go and look for your explanation?' "

Brink makes the motif of inversion, so powerful in the Song of Hannah and in the narrative of David, a powerful indictment of the "full" ones of South Africa who may end in emptiness. The situation upon which Brink comments in South Africa is not far removed from our own U.S. situation, where we also are full enough to gain the world, perhaps not empty enough to save our souls.

5

A Retrospect on Power, Providence, and Personality

In all the texts of David considered in this study, the narrative weaves a strange, artistic alternative to conventional notions of public power. Always and everywhere, the effects of power are taken seriously, sometimes celebrated, sometimes deeply critiqued. Always and everywhere, the person and personality of David are celebrated, enhanced, appreciated, and never diminished. Always and everywhere, the providential purpose of Yahweh is operative. Sometimes that providential purpose of Yahweh is a full commitment, as when Yahweh is "with David." Sometimes that providential purpose is as devious and hidden as "inciting" to a census in order to punish. Sometimes it is so hidden as to seem absent, as when the Philistine overlords do rescue work for David, in the seeming absence of Yahweh.

These three factors of *power, providence,* and *personality* have odd and unpredictable relations to each other. It is clear in each case, however, that the real story of Israel with David cannot be told unless the three factors all are taken into account. When we are excessively "managerial," we attend to sociopolitical power and do not notice often enough providence and personality. When we are excessively pious or ideological in our piety, we may only attend to providence and miss the significance and seduction of power, and the dazzling cruciality of personhood. When we are excessively "therapeutic," we attend to the person of David and tend not to notice power and providence.

Any of these excesses—managerial, pious, therapeutic—gives a skewed reading of the text, of our story, and of our life. Israel knows better. When we attend to these stories, we know better as well. These stories are not pious little exercises for children. In them we have a bolder, more complex, more dangerous, more subversive, more transformative story to tell than we can mostly tolerate. The telling of this story discloses how thin and dishonest are most of the stories by which we seek to live in a flattened world, so fearful of density, subtlety, and hiddenness. In the end, these stories matter, because without them we lose the capacity for a probing, imaginative, subverting alternative. We end then in conformity, despair, and brutality. Mother Hannah knew more than conformity, despair, and brutality. She sang better, and trusted more deeply; her life focused in liberated worship and moved to new public possibilities. We, like David, are her children!